Every Day Tao

Every Day Tao

Self-Help
in the Here & Now

Leonard Willoughby

Boston, MA/York Beach, ME

First published in 2001 by
Red Wheel/Weiser, LLC
P. O. Box 612
York Beach, ME 03910-0612
www.weiserbooks.com

Library of Congress Cataloging-in-Publication Data

Willoughby, Leonard.
  Every day Tao : self-help in the here & now / Leonard Willoughby.
    p. cm.
  Includes bibliographical references (p. 267)
  ISBN 1–57863–217–X (pbk. : alk. paper)
  1. Taoism.   I. Title.

BL1920.W55 2001
299'.51444—dc21   2001033322

Typeset in Adobe Garamond

Illustrations are by Leonard H. Willoughby, Sr.

Printed in Canada

TCP

08 07 06 05 04 03 02 01
8 7 6 5 4 3 2 1

The paper used in this publication meets the minimum requirements
of the American National Standard for Information Sciences-Perma-
nence of Paper for Printed Library Materials Z39.48-1992 (R1997).

To my teacher & to fellow travelers

Contents

Acknowledgments ix

Preface xi

Part 1 Tao—The Way 1
  1. Taoism 3
  2. The World 5
  3. The Journey on the Way 17
  4. Tint To: The Universal Law of Abundance 38
  5. The Law of Non-Infringement 63
  6. Good and Evil; Abundance and Infringement 76
  7. Tint To: The Universal Law (Continued) 79

Part 2 Te—Virtue (Integrity) 97
  8. Negativity and Your Reality 99
  9. Reality 101

10. Relationships and Your Reality 119

11. Self-Forgiveness 133

12. Love and Self Love 139

13. Celibacy and Sexuality 157

14. Taoist Mysticism 161

Part 3 Sam Ching (Three Realms of Being) **167**

15. Taoist Cosmology 169

16. Integration and Transformation 185

17. Taoist Thirty-Three Energies &
    The Thirty-Six Energies of Creation 211

18. The Eight Taoist Immortals 226

19. Create Your Own Mandala................................. 238

20. The Paradigm Shift from Matter to Spirit 248

21. Journey Back Home 255

Appendix I: Taoist Meditation 258

Appendix II: Advanced Meditation................................. 261

Appendix III: Meditation on the Four Elements 264

Bibliography 267

Acknowledgments

First and foremost my grateful thanks to my teacher Jeffrey Yuen who gave the teachings of the Way, and the encouragement for me to stand and become initiated in the Way. To Master Lu, priest of the Dragon Gate School who is a friend, and who introduced me to the Taoist Immortal Lu Dun Pin. To my friends Ed James who provided the circle of Yoruba Orisha and their Christian counterparts, and Muscat, who introduced me to Jeffrey. To my friend Anna Northrop, for her supportive, helpful feedback. To Mary Lou Sherwood, dear Sister Piety, for her input on Part 3 of the manuscript. Last, but not least, to the Taoist masters, deities, and Immortals, without whose help none of this would be possible.

Preface

When I became a spiritual seeker and tried to get an insight into spiritual life, I found it unclear and clouded in mystery until I turned inward to face the spirit. In my childhood years I was brought up as a Christian. However, in adolescence, I had many questions about the way, and found few answers. I began to look to Christian mysticism, Vedantic philosophy, yoga, and, more significantly, the teachings of Meher Baba. After eighteen years as a devotee of Meher Baba, by His grace, the internal path opened to me. He opened the way to the Hindu path of Krishna Consciousness, and Swami Pradhupada opened the way to Radha-Krishna. It was Radha-Krishna who opened the way from there to other deities of the Hindu, Buddhist, and

Taoist traditions—especially Tara and Avalokita, of Tibetan Buddhism, and Kuan Yin of the Chinese tradition.

As I entered a period of great difficulty in my life, compromising my spiritual practices, I sought a change of direction. I felt I needed a spiritual way of life that I could live in the every-day world. At about this time, a couple of friends who were a little further along the way than I told me about a young Taoist teacher named Jeffrey Yuen with whom they were studying in New York's Chinatown. I started going to his classes and after only a short time, I realized that his classes in Taoist philosophy, pressure point therapy, Chinese dietetics, Chinese herbal medicine, martial arts, etc., were all linked, not separate subjects. They all came from a place of a unified understanding within him. At the time, Jeffrey was about 22 years old. I wondered, "How is this possible?" I was amazed by his obvious spiritual maturity.

So I settled in to study the Way of the Tao. Although I was strongly attracted by Jeffrey's teachings, I found it difficult to apply some of them to my life—especially those dealing with transforming negativity and staying open to the energy of the Tao long enough to get the Universal Law operating in my life. Intuitively, I felt the truth of the teachings, so why did I find it so difficult to apply them? Jeffrey, aware of my difficulties and also of my previous connection with Kuan Yin, encouraged me to reconnect with Kuan Yin and seek assistance. About this time Jeffrey took our class to visit a Taoist Buddhist temple in New York City's Chinatown. The priest there performed for me the opening ceremony on two images I had of Kuan Yin, in order to bring into them the energy of the deity. Then, I began to relate to Kuan Yin as my ideal or higher self. It was after this that the way started to become more clear. I began to understand why I had so much difficulty. My teacher was giving the teachings of the Way of the Tao, from the place of the Tao, to us in yin/yang, the material world. I found it not only difficult, but also almost impossible, to step from yin/yang into the Tao. It was then that I learned that my teacher was partly raised by his grandfather, who was the Grand Master of the Taoist line. His consciousness was never really limited by his yin/yang material existence. It was then also that I realized he made the jump from yin/yang to the Tao in one step, but he was never really enmeshed in yin/yang. I realized I would have to make the jump in two steps. My first step would be from yin/yang, the material realm, to Tai Chi, the spiritual realm. This I would achieve with the help of my ideal and spiritual guide, Kuan Yin. I realized that a connection with the higher self is necessary to open up to the Way. Once this union with higher self is made, and the first step is achieved, travelers can take the second step into the Way. The Way of the Tao is within, it is the way of the mystic, the way of unconditional love or positive regard for all, lived out in the pragmatic world of the Taoist.

When I finished writing Part 1 and 2, I gave copies to whoever was interested, and my teacher gave some copies to his students. The feedback that came from his students was that they felt that they needed something more. When my teacher told me this, I realized what they were asking for, so I have added Part Three. This is how I pulled it all together to work for me.

To begin, many years ago, while I was living as a devotee of Radha–Krishna in India, I was given the task of writing down my realizations as my *sadhana*, or spiritual work. By writing down my realizations, pulling them together like beads on a string, they would ultimately bring me to an illumination that I could share with others. This gave me the teaching of integrating all the aspects of self.

Years later, while working internally with Kuan Yin Buddha to find out how to get the Way of the Tao to work for me, she pointed out certain connections. To begin, she pointed out that, as the eight trigrams of the Pa Qua represent all there is in Heaven and on Earth, they also represent eight parts of the self. Just as the eight trigrams, or eight subtle energies, came from the source, by balancing these energies within myself, I could return to the source. She hinted that it was interesting that there were the Eight Taoist Immortals or saints. Could there be a connection between them and the Pa Qua? In meditation on the Eight Taoist Immortals, I began to tune in to their energies and place them on the Pa Qua. When I finished, I showed Jeffrey what I had done. He made one correction and said I had it. The Pa Qua is very important, because it is like a road map. To know how we got here is to know the way home, to the source, to the One. For it is at the source that you come in tune with the Creator, and with your higher self as a manifestation of the One.

Taoism is a mystical path, the way is found within yourself. Taoists view the world as three realms of existence, or three grounds of being: yin/yang (this material world), Tai Chi (the subtle, or spiritual world), and Wu Chi (the source). There are definite lines of demarcation between these three grounds. They represent three different dimensions and are governed by different laws of being. So first you have to become united with your own soul nature, and linked up with your spirit or "I Am." Then you must come in tune with higher self and the Great Soul or Great Mother. This gives you sufficient purity of energy for your transformation. The way is to open the internal door of yourself by acknowledging the spiritual dynamic within your being, which is behind all material existence.

Self-realization came for me as a sobering experience. The realization that "I Am" spirit-soul; that I am part of the all-that-is. It was like waking up from a bad dream. I had spent my whole life looking for myself and seeking what I am supposed to do. Now that I have found my self, I know what I am supposed to do—share the way I found myself with others who are looking for themselves.

Coming into positive relationship with your higher self, one might say is prerequisite for true spiritual life; and is essential for a mystical path like the Way of the Tao. The Tao is both our Divine Mother and Father, the source of our consciousness and being. It is out of love that the divine grants us our sincere heart's desires. If that desire is for help in getting your spiritual life together, you should have no doubt about receiving help. Some call the divine:

Higher Self - Higher Power - I Am - God – Creator;
God Force - Spirit - Light – Universal Mind – Source;
Christ Consciousness - Cosmic Consciousness - Divine Love;
Earth Mother - Mother Nature - Terrible Mother;
The Great Soul - Great Mother - Mystic Female;
Goddess.

In this book, I use the term higher self to represent the God or Goddess within, with which we connect through our own spirit-soul. It is by functioning in harmony with higher self that we become the initiate and come into a positive relationship with the Creator. It is through our soul-self that we become connected to the Great Mother, with Her subtle network or pathways to Her inner dimensions and to all that is. It is Her energies that bring us into the flow of evolution. In the Way of the Tao we relate to deities not as divine beings outside of ourselves, but as spiritual energies to be experienced within our selves.

I refer to the energy of the Great Mother as the Tao of yin, and as it is the Mother's positive energy that influences our everyday lives, I call it Tao in the here and now. The energy of spirit, of the source of creation, I call the Tao of yang.

I use the terms Goddess and God in this book to describe the manifestation of the divine energies of the Tao of yin, and the Tao of yang, in creation. We need to acknowledge our own connection with these divine energies within our being, as aspects of the Tao within our selves, and within our fellow men and women, and all creation.

We have a spark of God within us, so we are heirs of the divine. It is our birthright to connect with the divine. All we have to do is ask to establish this connection in our lives. Each one of us has, deep inside our being, a Goddess or God, an aspect of the Tao, or spiritual energy, as though asleep, waiting to be awakened.

Those of you who would walk in the Way of the Tao, should get a good translation of Lao Tzu's *Tao Te Ching*, which will provide a philosophical base for your understanding of the Way. You can use the *I Ching*, along with the teachings of this book, as an aide in the practice of the Way. You may seek the guidance of the sage of the *I Ching* to inspire you until you gain a direct connection with higher self. Afterward, you can use the *I Ching* as a check on your internal intuitive perceptions. You can use books on the *I Ching* that are presented for self-help and spiritual growth, but not those that are designed for fortune-telling.

This is not just a book on Taoist philosophy. It is also a self-help workbook. In Part 3, I present a process of self-integration and transformation. As you live through this process, you may go back and forth through the book several times before you feel comfortable enough to move on. I recommend that you make a connection with your higher self as your guide, and confirm it with the Sage of the *I Ching* before you begin the process in earnest. Living through self-integration and transformation is an intensive process. So, if you come to a point that you don't understand, or cannot proceed further, stop and put the book down and come back to it some time later. Use this stopping-point for prayer, meditation, and reflection on the true nature of the reality before you and within you. Sincerity of purpose is the quality that will get you through. I also recommend that you read through the book first, at your leisure, to familiarize yourself with the teachings.

Then reread the book for understanding and the beginning of the self-help process.

This book is based on the teachings of the Jade Purity School of Taoism; given by my teacher, who as I said was brought up in the Taoist tradition. Realizing the value of the teachings I asked him to consider putting them into book form. He said he was too busy with other things, but that I should do it. That I should write from my own experiences, using my own words. This book is the result of adding my realizations to the essence of Jeffrey's teachings on the Tao, as well as my realizations from other Taoist and Interfaith sources. In writing I tried to maintain the spirit in which the teachings were given. Although the teachings are philosophical, they will have a devotional flavor, as my internal practice is the bodhisattva path with Kuan Yin Buddha, and internal contact with the deities. An advanced meditation given by Kuan Yin, in Appendix II, links the Way of the Tao to other Eastern and Western Systems for fellow travelers. I am presenting this book as an alternate philosophical system, springing from the roots of traditional Taoism. The teachings being presented are based on tapes I made of a series of classes on Taoist Philosophy, given by Jeffrey, between 1984 and 1989 in New York. My thanks to my teacher and friend, for initiating me into the Way of the Tao, and allowing me to pass it on.

PART 1

Tao—The Way

The Tao that can be told is not the eternal Tao.
The name that can be named is not the eternal name.
The nameless is the beginning of heaven and earth.
The named is the mother of ten thousand things.
Ever desireless, one can see the mystery.
Ever desiring, one can see the manifestations.
These two spring from the same source but differ in
    name; this appears as darkness.
Darkness within darkness.
The gate to all mystery.

—*Tao Te Ching*[1]

The starting point for understanding the philosophy of
Lao Tzu is understanding what he means by the Tao, or

---

[1] Gia-Fu Feng and Jane English, trans., *Tao Te Ching* (New York:
Vintage Books, 1972), chapter 1.

the Way. The Way is Lao Tzu's name for ultimate reality (though he continually points out that he does not know its true name, he simply "calls" it the Way). For Lao Tzu the Way is that reality, or that level of reality, that existed prior to and gave rise to all other things, the physical universe (Heaven and Earth), and all things in it, what the Chinese call the "ten thousand things" (wan-wu). The Way in a sense is like a great womb: it is empty and devoid in itself of differentiation, one in essence; yet somehow it contains all things in seedlike or embryo form, and all things "emerge" from the Tao in creation as babies emerge from their mothers.

But the Way does not simply give birth to all things. Having done so, it continues in some way to be present in each individual thing as an energy or power that is not static but constantly on the move, inwardly pushing each thing to develop and grow in a certain way, in a way that is in accord with its true nature.

That the Tao is a feminine reality and a maternal reality thus seems clear. It is not surprising, therefore, that Lao Tzu refers to the Tao as the "Mother" in no less than five places.

—Te–Tao Ching[2]

---

[2] Robert G. Henricks, trans., *Te-Tao Ching* (New York: Ballantine Books, 1989), p. xviii.

Taoism

In introducing the Way of the Tao to you, I must first speak about the culture of Taoism. Taoism reaches back to prehistoric times; there is no date allocated to it. Taoism is about the people being in harmony within themselves and with nature. It really means being in harmony with every thing around you. In ancient times, people began to adapt to and evolve in the environment they were living in. Their understanding or harmony with nature was called the Tao. All those who were seeking harmony within the self were considered Taoists. They pondered the questions of life and evolution. These were the people who became great thinkers, and brought to our world the teachings that I am presenting to you.

Around 600 B.C. there was a spiritual renaissance—not only in China, but also in all parts of the world—and great spiritual teachers appeared, offering transformational teachings. These teachings became the foundation for most of the philosophies and religions of the time. We know who they are because it was through them that we gained this understanding of how to be in harmony with ourselves once again. Among these great teachers is Lao Tzu, who was a vital part of the transformation that China was going through.

The Chinese acknowledge Lao Tzu as the founder of philosophical Taoism, which is a school of thought that reflects on nature. Lao Tzu's name translates as "Old Child," which shows us that life itself is a perpetual paradox. Lao Tzu's teaching in the *Tao Te Ching* presented people with a new way to think about themselves, life and the world around them.

Taoism is the way of surrender to the ebb and flow of nature as the way to fulfillment. It turned its back on the court, on statesmanship, and commerce, in favor of the silence and remoteness of meditation in the mountains. Tao means an understanding of self—self-cultivation, self-contemplation—it always deals with self.

The teachings I'm presenting are from the Yu Ching Huang Lao Pai, or the Jade Purity School of Taoism, which happens to be one of the oldest schools of Taoism. Its founders are Huang Lao, or Lao Tzu, and the Yellow Emperor. Now, as in the time of Lao Tzu, religions and philosophies are undergoing a renewal, and are bringing people through transformation into realization of self.

2

The World

Taoists represent the world as the Three Purities, or three aspects of ourselves. Three symbols are used to represent these three dimensions (see figure 1, page 6). These dimensions are internal. At the same time they are external. In relationship to Wu Chi, Tai Chi appears as darkness. In relationship to Tai Chi, yin/yang appears as darkness. To the Taoist, yin/yang, the conscious mind, this material world appears as darkness within darkness. So the Taoist walks in harmony with nature, to leave the darkness within darkness and come into the light.

Mystics speak of this dual darkness as two nights: the first is the dark night of the soul; the second is the dark night of the spirit. Shamans speak about the night and say that, in order to get through the night, you need an ally.

Wu Chi, Jade Purity, unconscious mind, group consciousness

 Tai Chi, Crystal Purity, subconscious mind

 Yin Yang, Grand Purity, conscious mind

Figure 1. Sam Ching—The Three Purities—Three Dimensions.

Mystics say you need a spiritual guide. Whether your ally is one of the archetypal forces of the shaman, one of the mystic's ascendant masters, or a deity or master of your own tradition, you may call on that energy to help you on your journey through the darkness into the light.

Grand Purity—
The Conscious Mind

Grand Purity is a dimension that is a window to the soul, but ego, or conscious mind, functions like a mirror. Its focus is on the external. Everything you see in the physical dimension is a reflection of your conscious mind. Everything you experience has been reflected back to the mirror. The way you feel about life, people, and the world around you, the things you think, say, and do, fashion the response you get back from life, and shape your reality. So you get from the world what you give to the world. The conscious mind's reflections draw to you everything, physically, mentally, emotionally. You attract to you the same vibrations you give off. This is the nature of yin/yang. When conscious mind functions as a window, its focus is on the soul. Using psychic abilities, divination (such as the *I Ching*), meditation, dreams, or Jung's centroversion,[3] you can access the soul and begin to tune into your higher self.

The conscious mind is like a mirror. It mirrors everything—physical, mental, and emotional—that you perceive about yourself. If you feel fear, it will mirror the fear and you will have fear coming to you. If you feel anger, it will mirror the anger and you will have anger coming to you. It reflects what you feel about yourself. If you feel you have an ugly body, it will give you an ugly body. Your conscious mind will reflect that image to you. Everything in your life is there because of you. You can say, "No that's not true," or, "When I was

---

[3] Centroversion is a process of self-reflection that an individual in latter years, around retirement age, naturally falls into, so one should prepare for it, and do it consciously.

young, my mother did this to me, and that's why I'm like this now." You can make excuses for many things, for many reasons about why you are, and who you are. But when it comes down to it, there is no one who can take the responsibility except you, even though, as a child, you may have been forced into a mold of negativity. So, to begin, you must accept yourself as you are and start from there.

Whatever you perceive about yourself, you automatically reflect it, like a mirror, and pull that vibration to you. There is a universal law that says, "Like attracts like." You pull to you the same vibration that you give off. Fear pulls fear; anger pulls anger; love pulls love. If you understand that, you begin to perceive how to break away from this thing we call the conscious mind. Remember that the conscious mind, in reality, is located in the brain. The subconscious mind, on the other hand, is an energy center within the physical body that exists beyond the physical dimension. Energy can never be created or distorted; it can only be transferred.

From time to time, each of us has said to ourself, "I am sick, I am tired, I am just really sick and tired of all of this." That is not true. You are not sick; your body is sick. You are not tired; your body is tired. Each aspect of self, indeed, extends beyond the physical dimension, beyond the body. The first stage of spiritual understanding involves getting beyond the body, and controlling it. It makes a big difference when you can say, "Well, my body is tired, but I'm not." So, if you have anger, it doesn't mean you have anger. Your subconscious mind is merely bringing the anger forth from you. That anger, in essence, is like a vibration released by the body, allowing an expression of energy. In essence, you are not really angry; a part of you that you have allowed to come forth is angry.

Crystal Purity—
The Subconscious Mind

Crystal Purity is everything that has been reflected in the mirror, everything you have experienced in this lifetime; it represents your soul, your personal reality. When soul, or subconscious mind functions as a mirror, its focus is on the external. The subconscious mind is like a computer program that contains everything you have allowed into your being. It is that which you have brought with you from the past. It also represents a blank wall at which you come to, yet can never seem to pass. It is the source of those things that haunt you and cause your imbalances. These imbalances must be reflected back from the mirror of your soul, back to your conscious mind, so that you can reflect on the content of your subconscious mind, reprogram it, and make yourself whole, as soul, as symbolized by the circle.

The circle represents the Pa Qua, the Taoist magic circle, similar to the Native People's Medicine Wheel (see figure 2, page 11). Its eight subtle energies symbolize eight aspects of creation and eight aspects of self. When you bring these eight subtle energies into balance within, you become whole as soul. When soul, subconscious mind, functions as a window, its focus is on the divine. When soul links with the divine as higher self or the Great Soul, it steps beyond yin/yang and becomes grounded in Tai Chi. There is no duality here, no good or bad, no right or wrong. Everything just is, and everything is perfect—the divine flowing through all.

Seekers and fellow travelers are constantly trying to understand more about themselves, but they frequently come up against a blank wall, something they can never seem to pass. The blank wall represents the obstructions within your subconscious mind, that keep you from getting beyond those things that haunt you, that instigate your reaction from a place below the surface of consciousness, and prompt your anger, your frustration, your prejudice, and your hatred. It is something you have allowed to be a part of yourself, something deeply rooted in the back of your mind. You live within it, and you are unable to get beyond it so that you find there are certain imbalances in your life.

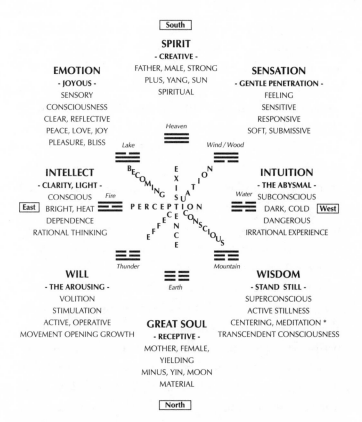

Figure 2. The Pa Qua. The Before Heaven Sequence of trigrams—the universal and creative mirrors the individual. As above, so below—as below, so above. Polar axes are from *The I Ching and the Genetic Code*, by Martin Schönberger (Santa Fe, NM: Aurora Press, 1979), pp. 52–55.

---

* See Appendix I on Taoist meditation.

You may have strong feelings about certain indiscretions of those around you that bring forth your anger. Perhaps you feel that those around you misunderstand you. You may find that your thoughts and reflections that lead you to take a new direction may be doubted or ridiculed by them. In dealing with that doubt or ridicule, you may have to relate to patterns that other people create. What they are really saying is, "What you are doing is not my reality, shape up and be like me." When you understand that, you understand that everyone's reality is very different. Everything that you see is perceived in your own personal way, because your subconscious mind perceives things in an individual way.

Some may feel very unhappy about their bodies. Some may be very concerned about money. Some may worry about finding a good husband, a good wife, or the right person for a partner. Every time you consciously think of something in your life that you lack, you have allowed that particular reality to become a part of you. If you feel fear because of "who you are," or "where you live," that fear attracts fear. So you have to become more conscious, not only of your thoughts, but also of your feelings and emotions. Remember, you attract the vibrations you give off.

You must also become more conscious of how you relate to others. If you ask someone, "How is your stomach?

Are you feeling better now?" you are acknowledging the fact that another person is feeling sick, and, thereby possibly amplifying their feeling of sickness. Words, and even thoughts, of affirmation have a very powerful effect on us. You may not realize it, but words can play a very significant role in your life. Each time that you communicate with someone you create energy vibrations. These energy vibrations can help, and they can also hurt. They can create balances, as well as imbalances.

As you become conscious of the energy vibrations around you, you realize that your soul or subconscious mind is an energy body. Crystal Purity is the dimension in which your soul becomes purified like a crystal and made whole. It is where you throw off the gross vibrations of the physical and open up to the spiritual energy or life force at the core of your being.

Spiritual energy is what we call Jade Purity. It is pure energy that has not yet manifested into the world. It is represented by a dotted circle, because energy is never confined, but is constantly in motion.

Although some of us may have what we call spiritual guides, they are not necessarily spiritual energy. Spiritual energy doesn't care about you. It only cares that you care about your self and, of your own free will, seek it, because spiritual energy, in essence, is the essence of what you are.

Everything through which you allow this energy to come forth is what we call "the vibrations." These vibrations represent the circumference of the unbroken circle; it is how you make use of the energy. Your vibration is the circumference that surrounds the energy and molds it to make you what you are. Everything you perceive about yourself is here, simply because you allow it to be. If you feel that you are poor, the subconscious mind says, "Oh, you feel poor, that means you should not receive." If you do indeed receive, you are going against your subconscious mind. Thus, when you say, "I'm poor," you'll find that you will be poor. If you say, "I'm sick," you'll find that you will be sick. The vibration derives from this energy, this circuit that is going out from the center of your being.

Like electricity running through a wire, it creates a vibration. The electricity travels through to the lightbulb, and you have light. That light is a vibration, or an output of the energy. Your subconscious mind is basically the energy that travels and creates the vibration, or what is called your conscious mind, the things that you perceive. In extending this further, you can say that your subconscious mind is much like your computer's memory. It is a storehouse that allows everything you experience to be contained within that area of your being. It therefore allows you to be you, but it also allows you to grow.

Jade Purity—The Unconscious Mind or Group Consciousness

Jade Purity is represented by a dotted circle, because it represents an energy of pure consciousness that can never be confined. When unconscious mind functions as a mirror, its focus is on creation. It's an all-knowing energy; it is pure, but impersonal. You must take an interest in yourself first, before it takes an interest in you. It moves through everyone and everything. When unconscious mind functions as a window, its focus is on the "One."

Jade Purity is that part of you that is separate from both the conscious and subconscious mind. In the West, this is sometimes called the "I Am" or Spirit; in Chinese, it is called the Tao. Spirit is the spark of spiritual energy that is the life force of your soul. It is the thing about which you know nothing, but which you want to come in contact with inside yourself. It is Spirit that remains after you shed your body and your mind. The essence of this energy is, in itself, formless. That's why it is called Spirit. It has no shape; it is not a physical being. Most people like to describe it as light. What better word can you use to describe energy? The "I Am" is, indeed, a consistent energy. It is something that fluctuates and perpetuates throughout eternity. It always has been, and it always will be. It's something that always flows through you naturally. However, because it is spontaneous, it needs channels through which it can express itself. It expresses itself through the body and through the mind. It allows you to learn more about yourself, within this thing that we call the physical dimension. You discover that the "I Am" that you are is something that works within yourself. It is your relationship to the all-that-is, through your relationship to your higher self, or Tao in the here and now.

This is not something that you can learn looking outside yourself. It's not something that you can receive by reading a book, or through observation. Spirituality is something that can never be taught. It is something that has to be deeply experienced, deeply felt by each individual. It is something that you find by searching within yourself. You may be able to find books that will spark this process. Indeed, everything that you use in this search is but a tool. This book, too, is like a tool—like a flint that can ignite a spark that you fan yourself. You create the fire; you ignite the spiritual energy within yourself. No one else can do that for you, because you are the Tao. You are the spiritual energy within your self, you are the "I Am." There is no such thing as an "I Am" out there that you reach out for. The "I Am" is in you already. If you reach *in* for it, it will be all around you. That's the essence of the Way of the Tao—to get to the point of understanding, and, going beyond understanding, to truly knowing, then going beyond knowing to simply being yourself.

3

The Journey on the Way

When you begin the journey to find your self, to know "who" you are, keep in mind that once you find out "who" you are, you won't be able to describe yourself. Spiritual energy can't be described. A true mystic, a true sage, is someone who acts, thinks, and speaks spontaneously. He doesn't think before he acts; he doesn't act before he thinks. Everything is natural around him. So, sometimes we have to work backward to come into that place. We have to work with the body to get to know it and go beyond its limitations. You can learn how to meditate, but meditation, in essence, is just a tool, not the answer in itself. We'll talk about nutrition, but nutrition, again, is a tool, not an answer in itself. There is no one thing that will lead to the ultimate. The ultimate is a synthesis of all things, because, once you reach it, you are all things. The Tao is in everything. In essence, you don't really need anything, you are all things. That's the paradox.

The Four Steps:
Four Disciplines of Self

There are four steps that begin the journey beyond the subconscious mind. You can begin with the step with which you feel most comfortable, but eventually, you will need to balance the four steps to come into the One.

Heart-Mind (Sum Yi)—
Working on the Emotional Body

Heart-Mind means that mind and heart are in harmony. Mind is the intellect and heart is the emotions, so your mind thinks about what your heart feels. Sometimes you think one thing, but your heart wants something else. So sometimes you make promises you later can't keep. That means there is an imbalance between your thoughts and your actions, your thoughts and your reactions. When you regain that balance, you gain control over your actions and your reactions. You also gain control of your creative, or ching, energy to manifest your creations in the world.

The first step of Sum Yi, or Heart-Mind, is known as thought-reaction, always saying what you truly feel. If someone asks you, "How are you?" and you answer, "Oh, I'm O.K." even though you don't feel O.K., your thoughts have not followed what you actually perceive and feel about yourself. People can know one thing and yet express another by their words when their minds are not in harmony with their hearts. The things they feel about themselves, or the things they feel about something or someone outside of themselves, are not in tune with what is actually going on around them. Whatever feelings you express, you have to mean them; you have to be able to actually convey what you feel inside. Remember, the subconscious mind does not accept, does not work with, the things you do not believe. If you do not believe it, your subconscious will not deal with it, because it knows you don't really believe it. It only contains what you have allowed to enter it. Your subconscious mind is everything you believe. In dealing with the subconscious mind, therefore, you have to remain conscious of this and only work with what you truly believe.

If you have a habit of saying, "I eat too much and I gain weight," and then you try to use an affirmation like, "I have a strong body, I'm not fat," to influence your subconscious mind and change that habit, the subconscious mind takes all of this information and says, "You don't believe that, because you always say you eat so much, so you must be fat." The subconscious always tries to tell you what you have already allowed it to be. It therefore always fights with you, with every thought, with every affirmation. Many spiritual teachings use affirmations because words are such a powerful energy vibration. They can create changes, as long as you truly allow the affirmation to be you. That's the only way an affirmation will work for you. If someone says, "I know you don't feel well, try to feel better," and you say, "O.K., I feel well," although you still feel sick, you will not feel well. The body doesn't work that way. You must truly believe what you say. You can't toss an idea into the air and hope that the subconscious will pick it up and put it into effect. The subconscious mind is what you have already allowed to be embedded into your reality. You therefore have to work solidly with all your thoughts and actions to bring about change. That's what we call Sum Yi.

Body-Mind (Shing Yi)— Working on the Physical Body

Some of you know Shing Yi from martial arts. Body-Mind means bringing your body and mind into harmony. If you can start to coordinate your thoughts and your reactions by stepping back and taking an objective view of yourself, you can start to deal with your body. In beginning to work with the body, one of the things you learn is the positive effect of using a psycho-physical discipline like Tai Chi Chuan or Chi Kung. When you perform a movement, you feel a tingling in your hands. You feel strength here, weakness there. You begin to understand a little bit more about your body, and begin to feel chi energy in your body. Once you realize you are not the body, the body comes out of the picture, and all you have to work on is the mind.

Shing Yi, or Body-Mind, is the second step of body reaction, or working with the body. Let's face it, most of us have had many terrible meals in our lives. Most of us have misused and misaligned our bodies in one way or another. The body says, "I like to eat meat, I like to eat sweets, that is what I'm used to eating." So we have to come to an understanding of why our bodies are as they are. "Why am I like this, why am I not like that? Why do I like to eat this? Why do I hate to eat that?" You begin to realize the value of food, you start to understand a little bit about what's going on in your body. When you eat meat, you should know whether your body accepts it or not. If your body accepts it, that's fine. However, first you have to find out if your body, in fact, does accept it. You have to take the time to check your body and see. Most of the time, we eat something because we like it, or just to fill an empty space in our stomachs. So, body reaction means we begin to rebuild the body. We begin to spend time each day, and actually feel the body. We learn to communicate with it, and know it, and not just use it.

When you practice Tai Chi Chuan or Chi Kung, you begin to realize what's going on in your body. That's the whole idea behind exercise from the Taoist perspective— to get you to learn a little bit more about your body. You begin to become attuned to your body. In essence, you begin to know your body, and really know what's going on with it. You begin to think about one part of your body, and how it will affect other parts of the body, because the body is one integral unit—it's a network of many parts all working together as a team, for the good of the whole. The heart doesn't work by itself; it works with everything else. The body is a whole being, working to express the energy within yourself. Now you can begin to get rid of all the negatives that you have placed on your body: how you look and how you feel. You begin to attune to your body.

You know that when you have a back pain, you begin to communicate with your back. In spite of the pain, you begin to identify with this hurting back. You begin to feel what's going on with it, and that identification eventually makes you have a very strong back. However, if you say, "God, it's painful," then you are trying to avoid the pain. You don't want to deal with it. You want to take an aspirin or whatever is necessary to get rid of the pain. But it comes back another day, and you still have to deal with it. So you deal with it now and you try to get in tune by using your thoughts and perceptions, and actually begin to feel your back. You ask yourself the question, "Why is this area hurting?" Then you start to allow energy to go into this area. The area will become stronger and stronger, because you are actually allowing energy to enter it.

In the same way, we can communicate with and heal all parts of the body, and all parts of the self. But first, we have to deal with the subconscious mind. An example: If you know a four-year-old boy named Jerry, and you tell him, "Your name is not Jerry, your name is Joe," the little boy will argue with you till the end of time that his name is Jerry, not Joe. Why? The child really believes what he has allowed himself to be—Jerry. Children believe very strongly in the things that have been embedded in them since they were born. The subconscious mind is in some ways like that child. It's very childish because it will argue with you about everything that you have originally given it or allowed it to be. If you say you are not, it will argue that you are, time and time again, until, finally, you begin utilizing affirmations and take control of your thought reactions. You can utilize control of your thought reactions to reconfirm or to reprogram what your subconscious mind originally believed. If you really believe what you are saying, you will have to allow it to be. Don't simply say, "I believe what I am saying." Believe what you are saying from within yourself. That's the only way you can get the subconscious mind to go beyond itself.

First, know your body. Begin to realize everything about it. Know where everything is in your body, and how the body functions—not by looking it up in a physiology or anatomy book, but by attuning yourself with your body. Close your eyes and look at your body, feeling the rhythm of your heartbeat, feeling the flow of your breath, feeling the floor connected with your feet, feeling the seat that you are sitting in, feeling what's going on in your body.

This shows you that you can go beyond the body, but you have to understand it before you can truly control it. If you put the blame for the condition of your body on someone else, saying, "Well it's because of such and such that I have this imbalance in my life," what you are really saying is that you have no control over your life. That's the reason why "such and such" can create such an imbalance in your life. With your higher perception, however, your identification with your body becomes a vibrating energy, because the body is a vibration. You can identify with it and heal it, because you understand there's a vibrating energy flowing throughout it. Once you understand that, you can extend it to other issues.

Pay attention to the things you put on your body, what you put into your body, and what you do with your body. Most of us have a certain taste in clothing. The clothes we wear should reflect who we are, and make us feel good about who we are. The things that we put into our bodies are very important also. Nutrition is important, because food is energy. Look at food as building and refurbishing the energy your body constantly needs. When you begin to look at the food you eat as energy, you begin to become in tune with the food you eat. It no longer just fills the empty space in your stomach. When you realize this, you truly begin to have control over your body. You may realize that, for example, when you eat Brussels sprouts, you get gas. You realize that if you eat purple cabbage, it really has the same energy as Brussels sprouts. If you can feel the energy of these two foods, you find they both have the same energy, and that by eating purple cabbage, you also get gas. You thus begin to know when you taste things exactly what they will do to your body, because you have become in tune with the foods around you. At the same time, you realize that you can go beyond your body, you can go beyond the food. Once you realize that, you're dealing with the mind, with something that's not physical. You cannot picture it. You can not grasp what is called the mind.

Dissolve Mind (Fa Yi)—
Working on the Mental Body

Dissolve Mind means to get the mind out of the picture. Some people think the mind is the brain, but, in essence, the mind is not the brain. It is a vibrational energy. By practicing meditation, you begin to go deep into the mind. Over the course of time, you open to Shen, or spiritual energy. This is the energy that opens you up to higher self in Tai Chi, or the spiritual dimension. It is from the position of Tai Chi that you can most effectively dissolve the mind. The mind contains the subconscious mind—all the things that have been programmed there since childhood. To go beyond the mind is to go beyond the relativity of yin/yang, and to go beyond Tai Chi. Tai Chi is represented as the symbol of the circle, standing for your soul self.

The third step, Fa Yi, or Dissolve Mind, is going beyond the subconscious mind. We have to begin with the conscious mind and work backward to the subconscious mind. The conscious mind is that of which you are physically conscious—your body, the clothes you wear, the food you eat, the people with whom you interact, your emotions, your mental processes. When you go beyond that, you go beyond yin and yang. Yin and yang means what? Relativity. You realize there is no definition for everything in life. There is no such thing as good or bad. There is no such thing as ugly or beautiful, because everything that we define becomes yin and yang. Everything we allow into our subconscious minds, in essence, is relative to who we are. If I say one thing is beautiful, it also means I automatically create something that is ugly. If I acknowledge that God exists, I automatically acknowledge the devil. To the Taoist, these seemingly opposite (by our Western standards) entities both represent a balancing of energy of the Tao.

The Tao is, in essence, the totality of all you can be. If all you can be is the totality of every thing, that means, in essence, that you are everything. You are good; you are bad; but there is no definition to it, because you haven't allowed that definition to be in you.

Other people can say, "That guy is crazy." Other people can say "What that person is doing is ridiculous," and sometimes we feel hurt by such comments. Sometimes when we get involved with spiritual teachings, we are ridiculed. Generally, we have a tendency to argue with those who ridicule us. Why? There is nothing to argue about if we realize that our reality is *our* reality, and their reality is *their* reality; and neither reality is better than the other. Why should we have to argue about one being better than the other? If they draw the sword, we don't have to come back and draw our sword and fight it out. There is no fight, because, in essence, spiritual energy is exactly what we perceive about ourselves.

If someone says to you, "That is silly. What you believe is stupid. What you believe is dumb," that's O.K. Just smile and walk away. You know within your self who is the crazy one.

So, in changing your thought pattern and perceiving spiritual energy within, basically you begin to change your perspective on your reality and begin to dissolve the mind. You begin to see all the relativity that has been placed in the physical dimension by which you have allowed yourself to be obstructed by. Once you can do that, you come to the last step. No Mind!

No Mind (Wu Yi)—
Working with the Spiritual Body

Once all the dissonant programs from the subconscious mind are gone, you no longer have to deal with the mind, and you become one with your higher self. Then you start to experience the Tao, the true self, who you truly are. You are in touch with spiritual energy, its pure energy that floats throughout everything around you. As an impersonal energy, spiritual energy—the Tao—only cares because you care. If you start to seek this miracle outside yourself, it will never come, because you have to acknowledge this miracle inside yourself before it can happen to you. For transformation, the process of becoming, is such that you have to be, then you can become. If you doubt it, or fear it, you have not allowed it to be a part of your life. The Tao is, in essence, the totality of all you can be. If all you can be is the totality of every thing, that means, in essence, that you are everything.

The last step is Wu Yi, or No Mind. You don't need to tackle the problem or the thought. You don't need to think about them anymore, because there is no thought, involved, there is no mind. When you reach that point, one of the major questions that comes up is are you ready to follow the flow? Are you ready to be natural? Are you ready to be spontaneous? This is usually a very difficult point, a very crucial step in leaving the mind. Most of us are not really ready to take that step. Most of us have a tendency to hold back a little bit of what we enjoy in life, not knowing that what we enjoy has been attached to us by the relativity that's been in our lives.

Everything you like in life is relative to you, so if you are still you, you are still attracted to the enjoyment. So when you reach no mind, the mind does not think about things because they are on your mind, your mind does not think about things because they are bad or good, your mind thinks about things simply because the mind is. It's a natural flow that's going through you. This recognition will allow for the dissipation of many of the crazy things that happen around you and that happen to you, allowing them to disappear.

So the real question is: Are you ready for your world, so to speak, to shatter in front of you? Your world, after all, has been created by the realities you have allowed over the years to be placed there around you. Most of us don't want to give up the reality we experience on a daily basis. By shattering our world, in essence, we shatter our minds, because our minds are our world. No mind, no world. This means spontaneity. Everything happens based on the flow; we just flow with it. That is spontaneity. We are here simply because we are here.

☯   ☯   ☯

There was once an old sage walking along a road. He came upon some students, who asked him, "Where do you come from?" The sage said, "I come from myself." "What are you doing?" the students asked him. The sage said, "I am teaching myself." Then the students asked him, "Where are you going?" "I will go where I will be," he replied. That's the idea of No Mind. You simply are where you are.

You simply are the flow, the spontaneity that's happening all around you.

❷   ❷   ❷

The more you become this thing we call the "I Am," the more you become the Tao, spiritual energy, the more you become reality in its entirety; not reality to be something; not reality to be someone else—reality, in essence, is everything that's going on around you.

How often, while walking along the street, are you aware of the cars going by? Are you aware of the people walking next to you? Most of us are so caught up in our own individuality that we basically live in our own little worlds. When we walk along the street, we are not really conscious of the street, except in fleeting moments when something catches our attention, or arouses our concern for safety. We are not conscious of the cars, or the people around us, because we are not conscious of a broader reality. Reality, for most of us, is a relative thing. It's what we do in our lives—the people, places, and things with which we interact.

No Mind is, indeed, a spiritual energy. It is an impersonal type of energy. It doesn't care who you are; it's a pure energy that floats throughout everything around you.

Nowadays, books are being written about spirituality, movies are being made about spiritual subjects, and people are more open about spirituality. If you have any apprehension or fear about spiritual living, those are things you have not allowed yourself to overcome. Spiritual energy simply does not care about the things you have not allowed yourself to overcome, because it does not care about you unless you care about yourself first. Spiritual energy only cares, the Tao only cares, because you care. That's the only way it becomes a part of you.

If you seek this miracle outside yourself, it will never come. You have to acknowledge that this miracle happens inside yourself before it can happen to you. The whole process of becoming is that first you have to *be*, then you will *become*.

You should come to understand the fears, doubts, and apprehensions you may have, because if you fear something, then you have not allowed it to be a part of your life. If you doubt something, you have not allowed it to be a part of your life.

All the great spiritual teachers were able to make this leap of faith. Some of you may say, "But that's dangerous. If we jump we might get hurt." That's true, but if you don't jump, how can you get to the other side? If you don't jump, how will you ever know? Sometimes you have to take that leap, even though you don't know what's going on. In his book, *The Universal Myths*, Alexander Eliot tells a story that illustrates this point well:

The Taoist philosopher Chang Tao Ling once led his three hundred disciples to the highest peak of Yun-T'ai. They saw before them on the far side of the mountain a fathomless blue abyss. Some 30 feet down the precipice, a slippery spur of rock jutted out into space; and at the point of the rock, a peach tree grew, its ripe fruits glowing against the backdrop of nothingness. "Which one of you," Chang asked his disciples, "dare to gather that tree's fruit?" One of them, a young man named Chao, dropped down to the spur of rock and ran out along it to reach the tree. Beneath it he stood plucking the peaches and placing them in the fold of his cloak, gathering one for each person present. Then he ran lightly back with his burden to the place where the rock spur joined the precipice, and tossed his peaches one by one up to the disciples and to Master Chang. The Master, leaning out over the precipice, stretched his right arm 30 feet down to help Chao climb up again, saying, "Chao showed courage. Now I will make a similar attempt. If I succeed, I shall have a big peach for my reward." With that he leaped from the precipice, alighting in the branches of the peach tree. He was closely followed by Chao, who stood in the branches at his right side, and by another disciple, Wang, who leaped and alighted at the Master's left. Chang spoke to the two in tones too low for the others at the top to hear what was being said. Suddenly, all three people, and the peach tree as well, vanished into space.[4]

The point of the story is, if you believe in your higher self, it will be. The whole idea of everything is belief—not belief in what other people say, but belief in yourself. Although we take the leap and sometimes we find there are tigers there, we have at least tried it. We have become aware that there are things that we have to deal with. It's like saying, "Turn out the lights and shut the door. Don't be afraid of any tigers that might be in the room." If you are aware of yourself, you will be aware of what's in the room. However, if you are afraid of yourself—which most of us are—and if you go within and close the door, you may be afraid, but what you are afraid of is yourself. Belief is going into yourself and saying, "I am what I am." Then you begin to find that abundance begins to flow around you.

One of the neatest things about being spiritual is being able to observe silence. We often talk about spirituality so much, we can talk it to death. If you can

---

[4] Alexander Eliot, *The Universal Myths* (New York: Penguin, 1976), p. 298. Copyright © 1976, 1990, Alexander Eliot. Used by permission of Dutton Signet, a division of Penguin Putnam, Inc.

describe it, it is no longer spiritual. Lao Tzu made it very clear, in the first chapter of the *Tao Te Ching*, the Tao that can be told is not the eternal Tao. The name that can be named is not the eternal name. If you can talk about it, it's no longer eternal. It's no longer spiritual energy, because it's really within yourself that you find the Tao, the true being of what you are. It is in your heart that you find your sanctuary, a place you can go for silence and the rejuvenation of energy. It's through silence that you really find strength. That's why meditation is indeed important; it gives you some time and space in silence. In physical silence, your mind begins to talk. Eventually, your mind starts to shut up, and then you can be at peace with yourself.

So now is the time for you to think about yourself. Do you really feel good about yourself? Not just mentally, but can you really see yourself, your body, the things you think, and what you do? Can you perceive yourself as being who you really are? If you can't, that automatically means you have stopped the flow, because energy is constantly flowing. If you deny your energy, or if you hate yourself, you cut the flow. Some may say, "This cannot be." Any time you say, "This cannot be," you have already stopped the flow. Believing means you begin to understand a little bit more about yourself. Think about how you perceive yourself.

This is usually hard, because we really have to start to face our fears, the doubts, frustrations, angers, jealousies, prejudices, and all those crazy things that we've allowed to be a part of our lives. We are, after all, what we pull to ourselves.

Remember, in the Way of the Tao, there is nothing impossible in the world, only impossible conditions that we allow upon ourselves. The impossibilities are what we have allowed ourselves to be, just as in Chinese medicine there are no incurable diseases, only incurable people. It is what we have allowed ourselves to be that has made us what we have become.

In knowing this, try to think a little more about yourself. Try to be a little more of what you are. Try to get beyond what you thought you were—because thought is still a thinking process—and simply become what you are. You'll find that spiritual energy remembers, and is only interested in you finding yourself—seeing the light within and seeing the beauty within, stripping it bare, so that you can truly see what's behind the light, what's behind all that you are.

In this way, you may see whatever struggle you have in this world, whatever it is within this world with which you have an imbalance. Maybe it's money; maybe it's your health; maybe it's your relationship. Whatever it is, you have allowed it to be. There are no accidents in this world, from the Taoist perspective, only what you have actually allowed to become a part of you. So you are never going to find answers outside; you will only find them within. You will not find the answers in this book; you will only find the answers by looking into yourself, searching within yourself, and believing in yourself. That's the only way. The Way of the Tao teaches: believe in what you truly are, and, once you start believing in yourself, you can truly be who you truly are.

Your Unique Way or Tao

There is a fifth step, or middle path, that is a synthesis of all four steps. This is found in the world, while living among your fellow human beings. This way represents how the four steps or ways come together in your life to form the fifth step or way. This fifth road is divine grace to you. It is your dharma, your own unique Way or Tao, how the divine, the Tao, chooses to manifest through you as higher self. This represents your life's work and destiny. To accomplish this is to do your dharma and fulfill your destiny, by fulfilling your role in the divine plan.

4

Tint To: The Universal Law of Abundance

The Universal Law of Abundance represents the Creator's Law of Love for creation. It is the masculine principle—the Tao of yang or the spiritual energy of unconditional love in the material world. When we live in harmony with the Universal Law, the energy of Tao illuminates our consciousness with the light of love.

You are the Tao, this magnanimous energy that exists and prevails in all things. This magnanimous energy continually maintains a balance, and everything that happens within our world is a balancing of this energy. Basically, it's a manifestation and an unfolding of this energy, trying to understand and express itself a little more completely. Coming into an understanding of this energy, and becoming a little more in tune with it is the Way. The discipline of the Way is coming into balance with, coming in tune with, the spiritual energy of the Tao. The best way to understand this discipline, in fact, is a discipline in itself.

To Understand Tint To

In Chinese, *Tint To* means the "Universal Law of Abundance," by which you can be all that you can be, because you are of the Tao, and the Tao is all-abundant. This Universal Law simply tells you that, as you are of this spiritual energy of the Tao, so you are all-abundant. Abundance consists of four keys, four realizations or approaches for coming into an understanding of self through the Universal Law.

In Buddhism, this is called the Four Noble Truths, although the Buddhist approach is slightly different. In the First Noble Truth, we recognize that the world consists of suffering. The Second Noble Truth says that our suffering is caused by ourselves, by our cravings and desires. The Second Noble Truth, within the Buddhist Way, is a recognition of the desires that are the cause of our suffering. The Third Noble Truth says that, once we recognize that these desires are the cause of our suffering, we can get rid of these desires, and thus get rid of our suffering. The Fourth Noble Truth shows us how to get rid of our desires. This last truth extends into the eightfold path of Buddhism.

The Way of the Tao is similar to the Buddhist way in that it consists of the Four Trues, which are comparable to the Four Noble Truths: True Mind; True Reason; True Virtue; True Tao. True Tao extends into the Pa Qua of the *I Ching*. The Pa Qua represents the eight trigrams, or the eight manifestations of subtle energy that help us to come into an integration of self. However, Taoists view the world from a different perspective. Taoists don't consider the world as suffering; they see the world as all-abundant. Everything can be a part of you and your world. Taoists let you know that you can have everything you want in the world. When you realize that you can have everything you want in the world, you ask, "Do I really need to have everything I want in the world?" At that point, everything becomes nothing, because it has no meaning if you know that when you have it, you don't really need it. Once you reach that point, it's the same as transcending what we call the desires. When you transcend your desires, you are able to adequately fulfill your needs and make your life complete, so you can be all you can be and fulfill your destiny.

The Four Trues

The first is True Mind or Right Identification
The second is True Reason or Right Involvement

The third is True Virtue or Right Manifestation
The fourth is True Tao through the Pa Qua

The Taoist Pa Qua, from the *I Ching*, represents the eight manifestations of subtle energy of Tai Chi. It is by coming into harmony with these eight subtle energies that you obtain true unity with yourself (see figure 2, page 11).

Conscious mind has much to do with our form and how we perceive ourselves. Our form is how we appear on the outside. It has much to do with our experiences in the world, our education, and our culture, with the outer or surface part of our lives. That's what creates our identities in the world, what creates the thing we call ego or false self.

We find that, no matter where we go and no matter what we do, there is always a tendency to measure ourselves by some kind of standard, or image, or a projection on which we can base our lives. There's always a tendency to measure and judge ourselves by something that's usually outside ourselves that helps us to align ourselves with the world. When we have to make a judgment call, we tend to find some means of comparison on which to base our decision.

When you look at yourself to see what kind of person you are, you gauge yourself by those around you. You use them as a yardstick against which to measure yourself. Your decision may be influenced by your group culture, by your education, by society, by some experiences you've had, or by some special group of which you are a member—by something we call form.

Any time you ask yourself something about yourself, you are trying to define something about yourself. When you do that, you are looking for some intuitive insight into yourself, some image, ideal, or projection that will give you a greater understanding of your life. You seek a fuller identity so you can have a greater involvement in your life, so you can reconnect with what's going on in your life at a deeper and more meaningful level.

As you seek this identity, you find that your outer form allows you to be something. Many times, because that something is outside of yourself, you find that you really don't know who you are or what you are to do. Some people really don't know who they are, why they are here, where they are going, or understand what's going on in their lives. They don't really have a sense of complete identity about themselves within this perspective.

Why? Because they are simply looking outside of themselves, trying to define their lives and give themselves meaning. Some of us do try to find out a little more about ourselves. The mere fact that we seek more of ourselves brings forth an energy we call Quest. We call upon this energy when we look into ourselves, when we try to understand and gain a more complete identity of self. This energy motivates us and allows us to be more complete.

Some people have trouble doing that. They constantly shift their images, their perceptions of themselves, and their definitions of their lives. They perhaps want to be like someone else they admire, so they take on their reflection. They take on the attributes or mirror image of that person. When they try to model their forms in the likeness of someone outside of themselves, they can't help casting a shadow on their own true natures.

If they are happy, their happiness is often based on what they perceive about someone else's happiness. One of the hardest things in life is to be happy. Why? Because we feel that certain attributes cause happiness, and therefore we lose touch with what actual happiness signifies inside ourselves—a sense of joy, of inner freedom.

When we seek abundance, we may seek physical abundance. Maybe we want a strong healthy body, one free of disease. We may seek emotional abundance; we may seek to experience, love, joy, and happiness in our lives. We may also seek mental abundance. We may want to have knowledge, to be able to convey our thoughts effectively. And what about spiritual abundance? Spiritual abundance is an area some people avoid. Why? Because, to be spiritually abundant, we have to work with ourselves. Most of the time, we don't really want to look at ourselves. We don't want to look at who we are. It's very easy to get someone else to take responsibility for our lives, thus we find spiritual growth or spiritual abundance very difficult to achieve. The only way to become spiritually abundant, the only way to be able to start on what we call True Mind or Right Identification, is to be able to say, "I know who I am, and I believe in myself." You have to really say it, and identify with it. Can you say, "I believe in myself," and identify with that as your reality? If you can't, that means you do not have a complete sense of your identity. You do not have a complete sense of who you are.

The Process of Coming into True Mind

What you are is not really you. What you are is what everyone else around you has allowed you to be. You are a vibration of other peoples' feelings, a vibration of the environment you are in. If you have fear, you probably live in an environment that promotes fear. If you have anger, you probably live in a situation, or work in a situation, or get involved in relationships, that promote anger. Whatever you perceive about yourself, you automatically reflect it like a mirror, and you pull that vibration to you. The

Universal Law says, "Like attracts like." You pull to you the same vibration you give off.

What happens when something bothers you about your identity? It has a tendency to take you places, to take you into situations in which you never know how you got there in the first place. It gets you into areas where you feel you are out of control. But if you look back, you'll see it's because you lost your sense of identity along the way.

You must start all over again, literally. This is the whole idea of the Universal Law; it shows you that you have to begin with yourself. You have to examine every aspect of yourself, including how you see yourself on the outside. If you feel lousy about yourself, chances are people around you feel that vibration as well. In understanding that, you begin to perceive how to break away from this thing we call the mind.

Remember that the conscious mind in reality is located in the brain. The subconscious mind is not in the brain; it is something beyond the physical dimension. It is a vibrational energy within your body called soul that never dies. So even when you die and lose this body that you're in, your vibrational energy continues.

The goal, therefore, is to break all of these vibrational energy patterns, to break the subconscious mind, so that you can begin to experience everything just as energy, seeing it for what it is, and not for what you would like it to be. What you are dealing with is energy, and energy is, in essence, impersonal. Energy is the central core of existence, and everything that projects out from it is a vibration. We have energy and we give off vibrations. In fact, what someone perceives about us is our vibrations. Now we want to cut the cord of all that in order to perceive the energy directly, no longer just the vibrations. When you no longer have to feel the vibrations, you can deal with the pure energy.

This Universal Law represents an energy of unconditional love from the Creator or Tao. Your ego or false self is the veil that obscures you from your true self and from experiencing this energy directly. We feel we need to function like this because we tend to follow the flow. That flow, however, is an external flow, and not the actual flow of energy. And what we are concerned about is energy.

If you are this spiritual energy, if you are this life force some call Cosmic or God Consciousness, or the Tao, how are you going to relate to it? If you do relate to this energy, it really doesn't matter what you call it, as long as you realize that this magnanimous energy that we call Tao is, indeed, all things. Whether you find it in nature, in the flowers in spring, or in the world around you, you become open to it and identify with it.

Right Identification means to identify with yourself, to begin to understand and know a little bit more about yourself, literally to try to transcend yourself and become open to higher self. That's the process you're going through. If you really ask yourself the question, "Who am I?" you'll find that's what leads to True Mind.

True Mind or Right Identification

Who are you? Well, you are the Tao. You are the life force we find within all things. If you can recognize that you are this life force that we call the Tao, that means that everything is available to you, because the Tao is in everything. If the Tao is in everything and you are of the Tao, then everything is in you and everything is available to you. With a little discipline of self, you can be a part of everything that there is in this world.

Consider how many of the things that went on in your life today were a part of your reality and how many were initiated by someone else's reality. This can tell you how much control you have over your own life. If you can say everything that happened today was a part of your reality, then you have complete control over your reality. The world you see is basically a perception of yourself. Everyone has his or her own reality. There is no such thing as a true reality or an absolute way. We each create our own reality.

We have to try to understand that no matter what our reality is, it's just energy. So, in reality, our reality is an illusion. It doesn't really exist, because we are energy. How we allow the vibrations of our energy to display themselves is the illusion of its manifestation.

To better illustrate this point, I will relate a story that may give you a better perspective on some of the things I've been talking about. This is a true story about a sage who lived in China long ago.

There was once an old sage walking the roads and paths of China, for what seemed like endless years, but each year was a very different one. There were new villages, new people, new students, and new experiences. There were constant changes going on, and life never seemed to be the same. He came to a village by the sea and there, a little boy came forth. The little boy asked the old sage to accept him as a student. The old sage looked at the boy and said, "Yes, you may travel with me. Together we may try to step beyond all that we can see."

They had not journeyed far when they saw a dead bird on the roadside. They continued a little further along the way, and they came upon an injured deer bleeding along the road. The student said to the sage, "Let's stop and tend to the deer. Let's give it healing and help it." The sage said, "Why?" The student said, "Because you must be kind to all living things." The old sage again said, "Why?" The student said, "Because that is what we are here for. That is what the great Tao says." "The great Tao doesn't say that," said the sage. "The great Tao says, 'what is isn't, and what isn't is.' First you must understand that pain in general is that which you have yourself perceived within the physical perspective in your world, and that pain is a subconscious alignment to the reality that you have, because you have identified with the physical world. So everything that exists in the physical world that you identify with affects you."

The words were new, and the student was confused. He said, "You are just going to let that animal lie there and die." "No," said the sage, "I didn't let the animal lie there; the animal was already there before we came. One of the things you must learn is to be able to perceive all things, to be a part of all things, you have to stop being a part of one thing. You have the ability to see beyond what seems to be, to perceive its expression, to feel its vibrations. Now you have to try to see or perceive its energy. The way to perceive it is to observe it, not to judge and criticize it for what it is and what it is not, because of what you are or what you are not. You have to learn to observe."

The student scratched his head and they went ahead in silence. Finally, they made camp and both fell asleep. The next day along the way, they came upon two small armies fighting one another. Blood was flying here and there, guts were spilling, and heads were falling. The sage and the little boy stood under a tree watching. The student was moving back and forth, pushing his arms this way and that way, reacting to those who were falling, moving as if his arm were a sword. He was deeply involved. He looked at the sage, who had no smile and no sparkle in his eyes. When one army fled, the other took off after them. The student asked the sage, "How can you just sit there? Those that ran needed your energy, those that ran needed your help." The sage said, "How do you know those that ran were not the robbers, and the others were those who were carrying the money? Do you choose to side with those who are weak, because they are weak?" The student said, "I don't know." The sage said, "Why do you identify with those that are losing?" The student said, "Because they are weak and the weak need help." The sage said, "Does help strengthen them? Or does it reinforce their weakness? Those that give the weak help make them weaker."

"Then let us tend to those that are bleeding, those that are dying," said the student. "Those that died, let us bury them." The sage said, "Why?" "That is the right thing to do," said the student. The sage said, "Why didn't you bury the dead bird along the road?" The student said, "That was just a bird." The sage said, "It was a living thing." The student said, "You said last night not to stop and care for those." "Those what?" "Animals," the student replied. "What's the difference between the bird, the deer, and the men?" The student said, "You can communicate with a man. You can talk to a man. You can have a relationship with him. You can give support to and strengthen a man." "In other words," said the sage, "you have levels of comprehension, levels of awareness of empathy. You can, on one level, be considered righteous, and, on another level be considered cruel."

Now the student was even more confused. As they walked away, leaving the dead and the injured, the student heard the cries of the injured in their pain, and he was truly upset. What to do? The little boy felt he had aligned himself with a sage who had no feelings. He was going to travel with an individual whom he feared, who did not help anyone. They had traveled for two days and they did not do anything. They did not help anyone. They did not save anyone who was hurt. They did not provide strength to anyone. They hadn't done any good deeds. They hadn't acquired any merit.

As they came to the top of a hill, they saw a pack of wolves running down a deer. The wolves killed the deer, tore it apart, and ate it. The student said, "How could you stand there watching that terrible thing?" The sage said, "Whose side are you on, the wolves or the deer?" "The deer," said the student. "It would not hurt the wolves; it would not give them any problem." "That is your perception," said the sage. "Why do you eat the chicken and the corn?" The student said, "Because it is good." The sage said, "You don't think that the wolves would think that the deer was good?" The student said, "But that was a living thing." Then the sage said, "Are the chicken and corn that you eat dead things?"

The student's head began to spin. Everything he had learned was being turned upside down. The sage said, "Let old thoughts pass away. There's one thing about the world and that is that everything is evolving, everything is balancing. Every kingdom has balance within the imbalance. The carnivores within the herbivores, all the kingdoms except man, instinctively know how to regulate and balance energy. Only man cannot maintain harmony within himself. If someone says, 'I'm sorry about that,' that just amplifies the hurt." The student said, "But an animal is not intelligent, an animal does not know what..." And the sage stopped him with a stare. "Who says you can speak for an animal? Who says that an animal is not happier where it is? You have to stop putting people and things where you think they should be."

That night, they sat around the fire for warmth and ate. The sage handed the little boy a quince and said, "Here, eat this." The student made a face and said, "I don't like quince." The sage said, "Why?" The student said, "I don't know, I just don't like it." The sage said, "Does your mother like it?" The student said, " I don't know." "Does your father like it?" "I don't know." The sage said, "When was the first time you can remember not liking quince?" "I don't know." The sage said, "Do you like rice? Do you like corn?" The student said, "Of course I like them." The sage said, "Then why don't you like the quince?" The student said, "My taste buds don't like it." The sage said, "Ah, now we are getting somewhere; your taste buds don't like the taste." "Yes," said the student. The sage said, "Ridiculous. You're saying your taste buds are controlling what you eat and don't eat. Or do you control your taste buds?" The student didn't really know why he didn't like it. Then the sage said, "Everything that you like or dislike has been placed there by a feeling, by an experience, by an observation of others, by some deep feeling or emotion.

"Do you really see what you see?" the sage asked. "Look at the fire. Can you feel the fire?" The little boy said, "Yes, it feels warm." "Can you smell the fire?" "Yes, I can smell the burning wood." "Can you hear the fire?" "Yes, I can hear the crackling." "Can you taste the fire?" "I feel its warmth in my mouth." "Now," the sage said, "that fire has become an experience. It has become an experience within your five senses. It has become something that has been placed within your subconscious mind." Then the sage got up and disappeared into the woods. The little boy fell asleep. Upon waking, he still didn't see the sage and waited. After days, the sage still did not appear. Finally, one evening, the little boy decided it was time to continue on, and he left. After the boy left, the sage came back to the campground and sat by the weakening fire. He said, "It's always so easy to learn from others, but it's so hard to learn from oneself. The power is in you. The way to find it is to accept it. And the way to accept it is to believe in yourself. And the way to believe in yourself is to know that you are the Tao." And the fire got stronger again.

ory gives you a perspective on evolution. It gives
strong perspective, for that matter, on under-
why people have a tendency to want to quantify,
to judge, to criticize, and to isolate everything into neat
packages so they can categorize it and give it a place in
relativity. This is good; this is bad; this is right; this is
wrong.

As you begin to understand Right Identification, you
begin to identify with yourself for what you are—not
for what you feel is right or wrong, but simply for what
is. If you cry and say, "Life is terrible," that means the
life force within you is not conscious. You are not allowing the totality of what you are to be expressed
through you. If you have restricted your own reality,
then you simply cannot have things the way they should
be, because you have restricted yourself. You haven't
extended to what we call the "livingness" of all other
things.

You need to identify those things in your everyday life
that are constantly trying to stop the flow of your abundance. For example, if you feel very insecure about money,
if you feel very insecure about your life's direction, if you
feel there are things in your life that are not allowing you
to express yourself completely, you have allowed them to
restrict the flow of yourself. You have restricted your own
life force.

You must start by understanding that evolution carries this life cycle. It is the flow of life energy of the Great Mother—what we call the Great Soul—that runs through all creation. It is the process of change that gives life and form to all in creation, and the possibility of transformation. It is the thread of existence, like a giant network that holds all creation together for the evolution of all in creation. Likewise, we are trying to come into harmony with, and to better understand, evolution, so we can become open to its cycle, so we may come into its flow.

It's very easy to go to a therapist, or a spiritual teacher, or a guru, and ask them to solve your problems. In reality, they are not solving your problems. They are giving you a different perspective from which to view yourself. You have to go into your own self to find out who you are. That's the only way. Why? If you feel you have such a difficult time now feeling the life force inside yourself, how can you possibly find it? That's why we have a tendency to look outside, a tendency to go somewhere else to find the solutions to the problems of our own reality.

When you say, "I want to gain good health," good health is something that you perceive and that you maintain. Good health does not last forever unless you maintain it. There is always a maintenance factor. That's what evolution is— the maintenance of energy. It's an on-going process. You don't gain evolution, you don't gain spiritual energy, you maintain it. You perceive it first, and, if you can perceive it, you can maintain it. If you feel sick, you must first be able to feel that you are healthy. Then you can maintain health within your body. Likewise, you must first perceive the life force, the Tao, within your body as spiritual energy. Then you must maintain it.

True Mind is Right Identification with your true self. It is from Right Identification with your higher self that you come into the flow of Tao, that pure consciousness that awakens you to your life's work and your destiny. In doing your life's work, in serving others, you will feel happy and fulfilled. You come into your own good fortune by helping others find theirs. You can know how to do that best by checking your own gut feelings, by tuning in to the emotions of your heart and the guidance from your higher self. True Mind begins when you realize you are the Tao, you are this life force or spiritual energy within all things. So everything is available to you, because Tao is literally in all things. If Tao is in everything and you are of Tao, everything is in you and available to you.

Right Identification begins when you identify with yourself for what you are—the Tao within—and not for what you were taught, the things within the program of the subconscious mind. First, look at the things you like and the things you hate to gain an understanding of all the things that bother you, in order to better know yourself. Then you can gain a sense of identity about who and what you are, and why you are here. As you come in tune with your higher self, you become aware of your own unique talent or calling. When you realize your unique talent and utilize it to serve others, you experience the joy in serving. For when you are working from your higher self, the spiritual energy brings you into the place of Tai Chi, where time seemingly stands still, and you enter into a state of timeless awareness. This is the place where inside and outside meet. From here, you come into an understanding of spiritual energy.

True Reason or Right Involvement

True Reason represents a more detached attitude to the things of yin/yang. With True Reason, you don't give up the things you need or the work you have to do, you give up your attachment to the results. As you open to your higher self, you become open to Universal Mind. The things you need to make your life complete become attracted to you through your sincere faith in the power of your higher self. In functioning from this consciousness, you fulfill all your needs. When you take the precarious step into the obscurity of the abyss, the great womb of the Mother, you open up yourself to the infinite resources of the Tao for your highest good. In this enigmatic place of the Great Mother, you find the space to wait for answers to emerge, through the chaos and confusion, from higher self. It may take some time for you to get the Universal Law operative in your life, so persevere.

Right Involvement asks, "What is your true reason for serving others?" True regard or love should motivate your reason, so that you work in positive relationship with the Universal Law. Rightly handled, Right Involvement will bring you to the place of co-creator, the place where you can transform your reality. Now that you identify with the Tao and know that all things are part of the Tao, you also know that you can be a part of all things. The Universal Law of Abundance tells you that, if there is something that you need in order to express your self in the world more completely, that something will come to you. Right Involvement means that subject and object are in harmony, and are starting to vibrate together, slowly pulling together to attract the object to you. But you find that to come into Right Involvement, you must be in tune with your true self and with your environment. You must know how the things you pull to you will affect you and your environment to make your life complete. You have to let the things you pull in be a part of you. At the same time, you have to be a part of them. That is completion—the object and the subject becoming one. You must understand what's happening around you and how each thing you pull is going to be an extension of you, a manifestation of you.

You are then able to pass on the abundance, because you realize it's free-flowing.

True Virtue or Right Manifestation

True Virtue means right follow-through with your service and resources for the benefit of others. When you do self-less service, you find you expend less energy working in harmony with your higher self. You find that things come more easily when regard or love motivates your actions. When you allow money or personal gain to be your central focus, you cut the flow of energy to you and interfere with the manifestation of your abundance. As you refocus on your life's work as your spiritual calling and offer it to your higher self, you come into True Virtue. You find that everything you align yourself with is energy, everything you own is in vibration with you. There is a livingness in everything you have, and it should be expressed in your life and in your work. Then the Universal Law of Abundance will manifest in your life.

Right Manifestation is based on working in positive relationship with the Universal Law, which represents the flow of creative energy in creation. This energy flows through all things, and if the circulation of this energy is stopped, life comes to a standstill. In Tai Chi Chuan, as you begin to work with energy, you learn that you have to push down in order to jump up. You have to push back in order to move forward. So there is a need to give out, to make room to take in. The greater flow out makes room for a greater flow in. However, it is the motive behind your giving and receiving that is of paramount importance. For if you have any attachment to what you give, there is no real flow of energy. The energy remains with you, and not with what you gave, so it is not truly given. If you want to manifest the things you need to make your life complete, help others get the things they need to make their lives complete. It is in the selfless service of your fellow human beings that you find the Way. Then you will be in harmony with your true self and with your environment, and the things you need to make your life complete can manifest in your life, and you can utilize them as an expression, a conveyance of you.

Anyone who just sits at home and prays for things, or thinks that things will come to them without an active involvement on their part, is laboring under a delusion. There has to be an active involvement on their part, and the things they need have to convey what is true mind for them.

True Tao

True Tao is freedom from attachment to the things of yin/yang. You can have them and use them to make your life complete, while not being attached to them. Attachment is the insecurity that will pull your consciousness back to yin/yang. When you discover your essential nature and know who you really are, you develop the ability to know what your life's work is and how to fulfill your destiny.

If you could have everything there is in this world, what would you do with all the things that can manifest in your life? Will you use them, misuse them, abuse them, or are you going to make your life complete? How are you going to involve yourself with the things that are pulled to you? You literally have to know who you are; this is True Mind. You have to know the things that will make your life complete and why; this is Right Identification. You have to know your environment, you have to know your connection with and your relationship to everything around you; this is True Reason. You have to know how you will use these things; this is Right Involvement. You have to know that everything you manifest will be used for the benefit of all; this is True Virtue. And you have to know how these things you manifest in your life are going to affect those around you; this is Right Manifestation. With the unfolding of this energy that you pull to you—the vibrations, the manifestations—how is it going to affect the people around you? It requires a direct involvement; it involves a deep, complete commitment. Subject and object become one True Tao.

The Universal Law Is the Creator's Law of Love

We are all manifestations of the Great Mother and Father that the Taoists call Tao. Everything we request sincerely from the heart—where karmicly possible—the Creator will grant out of love. To teach us how to live in harmony with this law, the Creator has given us the law of Non-Infringement, or the Law of Karma, so that we may learn how to bring our lives into balance. As we start to live in harmony with this Law, we go through spiritual transformation and become helpers in establishing the Creator's divine plan on Earth. By working in harmony with the Universal Law we can have abundance. We can also work with the Universal Law to free ourselves of ego or false self, to transcend desires, and to transform pain and suffering in our lives. Through this enlightened attitude of mind, balanced by love from the heart, we can manifest a new reality. To understand how to work with the Universal Law to transform our lives, we first have to understand the Law of Non-Infringement.

The Law of Non-Infringement

The Law of Non-Infringement represents the Way of the Mystic Female—the feminine principle—the Tao of yin, the Great Mother's force of love in the material world. It represents the force that brings the reactions to our actions—those things we say and do to one another that come back to us with love (the Great Mother's grace) to teach us how to love. When we live in harmony with the Law of Non-Infringement, Her energy fills our being with love.

Mankind has been given free will by the Creator, the source of all creation. This is acknowledged through the Universal Law that says you can be all you can be, because you are of this life force. In the practice of the Way, in order to acknowledge our own divinity, we must acknowledge the divinity of our fellow men and women and of all creation. We do not have the right to impose our will on others without their understanding and consent. That is infringement. If others consent to accept our advice or do our will, then that is not infringement, that is affinity— our working in harmony with others. When you admonish a child, a loved one, or a misguided person for something that you feel is for their own good, although it may hurt them, that should not be considered infringement, because you are doing it out of a feeling of responsibility to them and to yourself. Acting out of responsibility is not infringement; it is an expression of love that will gain love.

However, if we see what we think is a fault in our brother, we should not seek to fault our brother, but seek to correct the fault first inside our self. For as long as we are looking to see the faults in our brother we can never see the divine. We've become so programmed to seeing faults that we can't see the divine. We have to first reflect the program of seeing faults in others from the subconscious mind back to the conscious mind and reprogram ourselves to only see the divine. We can only do this with the help of the divine, our own higher self. We will then be ready to willingly take the bitter pill of strong medicine from the divine, for our purification, for our transformation. This change of vision eventually lifts us out of the realm of yin/yang, or Grand Purity, and establishes us in the realm of Tai Chi, or Crystal Purity. It is this change of vision that enables us to be of true help to others. At this point, we can truly speak and act to help our brother, because we aren't acting out of self-centered reasons or negative emotions, but acting out of sincere regard or love.

Those who are ignorant of who they are and why they are here, and don't utilize the Universal Law to work for them in a conscious way, will find that some part of it works for them, but in an unconscious way. Instead of it working to free them from the bondage of the material world, it grants them some small portion of their hearts' desires, but it also pulls to them their fears, which cause them pain and suffering.

Every time we break the Law of Non-Infringement, the quality of our energy is altered or colored by the nature of our digression. What then is necessary is to seek forgiveness and make a sincere repentance and try to gain an understanding of the mind, linked with a complete change of heart. This will free our hearts from the grip of self-serving desires and negative emotions, and open us up to love. We can then begin to reestablish our connection with the Universal Law. A complete change of heart is necessary to bring about a purification of our energy. That is why transformation is considered as going through a dark night of the soul, or purgation. It is a purging and cleansing process that turns our selves inside out—cleansing our hearts and opening our minds, bringing the two into harmony so that they may become one.

To some people, Taoists seem to be pacifists, but this does not mean they condone infringement. It's not that Taoists ignore infringement or do nothing about aggression, but rather, by their words and deeds, they try to show that there is a more enlightened way of functioning. If this fails to spark a change in aggressive attitudes, as a last resort, they may take corrective measures directed by higher self, to return things to normal as quickly as possible. To begin with corrective measures would be to infringe on the infringer.

You could say that the Law of Non-Infringement is the other side, or the shadow side, of the Law of Love—the Universal Law of Abundance. Most people see them as two distinct Laws, but, in truth, they are two aspects of one and the same law. This is vividly illustrated in the Hindu path, in the worship of Shiva and Shakti. Shiva represents Spirit, the creative force of God the Father. Shakti represents the nurturing force of God the Mother. Shakti is represented by the Goddess Parvati's feminine energy, which has two main aspects—Mahamaya and Yogamaya.

As Mahamaya, or material energy, Her energy censures and disciplines Her children that they may know how to live and love. Taoists call this the energy of Non-Infringement.

As Yogamaya, or spiritual energy, Her energy works positively to help spiritual seekers on their way to transformation. Taoists call this energy the energy of Quest.

This is an interesting phenomenon. It seems as if the Great Mother has a loving side and a wrathful side, with many shades of gradation in between.

The teaching in the Hindu Way says that it is the nurturing role of God the Mother to guide us to have only right desires. Only then can we become open to the grace of God the Father, which is Spirit, because God the Father must satisfy all other desires that can be satisfied before He can give us His grace. If God the Father gave us the grace of Spirit first, all our other desires would be left unfulfilled.

In the way of the Tao, you begin by establishing True Mind, by coming into alignment with your higher self in order to know your true self. You can then come into right identification with the world around you, and begin to come into harmony with the Universal Law. As you tune into the Way with all sincerity as a seeker, that opens you to the energy of Quest, of the Great Mother. It is Her energy that opens the way to the realm of Tai Chi and Wu Chi. It is the yin energy of the Great Mother we call the Tao of yin that brings you into union with the yang energy of the Creator, which we call the Tao of Yang.

The valley spirit never dies;
It is the woman, primal mother.
Her gateway is the root of heaven and earth.
It is like a veil barely seen.
Use it; it will never fail.

—*Tao Te Ching*[5]

The Great Mother's energy is yin, as it represents the feminine principle. In relationship to yin/yang, however, it is yang, or divine energy, because it is from the realms of Wu Chi, via Tai Chi, and represents the Tao in the here and now.

The Great Mother's energy forms a network of the Tao of yin throughout creation. As the Taoist mystic female, this energy gives life, and nurturing to the ten thousand things. This energy is the active energy of the Tao that flows throughout, linking every aspect of creation with the Tao. The energy of Spirit is the passive energy of the Tao of yang, and it is the ground in which this creation has its being.

Hindus see the material world as the realm of Mahamaya, or the ocean of Maya, or illusion. One has to cross over or dive deeply into the ocean of Maya, until one comes to the other side.

---

[5] Gia-Fu Feng and Jane English, trans., *Tao Te Ching* (New York: Vintage Books, 1972), ch. 6.

Taoists see the material world of yin/yang, as the realm of darkness into darkness, because, in the dimension of yin/yang, we only experience the reflections of the sub-conscious mind. As a seeker, you can come into positive relationship with the Great Mother's energy of Quest and then dive deeply into the subconscious mind, the realm of the Great Soul, the mystic female, who then becomes your guide and protectress.

It is like diving deeply into yourself, and becoming open to your soul-self as your energy body, and opening up to the universe as an ocean of energy. You find you are one with all others, and all others are one with you. Everyone, to some degree, shares the same experience of the livingness of being. When the soul, through your higher self, is in tune with the Great Soul, it gradually becomes open to the realm of Tai Chi. Tai Chi is the place where the soul communes with and becomes an instrument of the Great Soul and Spirit. As you become open to the Great Soul, let Her be the player and you the observer, until you learn how to play also.

The first experience of Tai Chi is very subtle. It comes as illuminations, or as openings into a new, more sensitive place within yourself. This awakening is in your sense of being and opens up your feeling nature. This is the trans-forming effect of the energies of the Great Mother that unclog the meridians and get the microcosmic orbit circulating. This energizes the three tan tiens, opens the psychic centers or chakras, and gets their wheels spinning. This represents the center channel, or the mystical sword or rod that you must seize to come into the flow of shen or spiritual energy.

To help us get into Tai Chi, the Great Mother helps us get beyond fear by revealing to us our true nature. The teaching given is that it is the quality of your energy at the time of transition that some call death that will determine where you go when you leave here. When you know this, you have no more fear, as your fear is of the unknown. Once you know who you are and where you are going, there is no more need for fear.

> The beginning of the universe
> Is the mother of all things.
> Knowing the mother, one also knows the sons.
> Knowing the sons, yet remaining in touch with the mother,
> Brings freedom from the fear of death.
> Keep your mouth shut,
> Guard the senses,
> And life is ever full.
> Open your mouth,
> Always be busy,
> And life is beyond hope.
> Seeing the small is insight;
> Yielding to force is strength.

Using the outer light, return to insight,
And in this way be saved from harm.
This is learning constancy.
                    —*Tao Te Ching*[6]

As twenty-four hours is a cycle in time, as the passing of day into night represents one day in our lives, so the passage of the four seasons represents a cycle in time that forms our year. Likewise, the cycle in time that forms the four seasons of our lives—from birth to youth, from youth to maturity, from maturity to old age, and from old age to death—represents a larger cycle in the time we spend here. How we relate to life will determine what kind of attitude we have about time, death, and transition. To the wise, a lifetime is like a day in the life of one's spirit-soul, and death or transition is like a night. The spirit-soul lives many of these days and nights, until it is ready to move on.

The Law of Karma and The Law of Energy Response

The Universal Law says, "Like attracts like." You pull to you the same energy vibrations you give off, because energy that vibrates at one frequency pulls energy that vi-

---

[6] Feng and English, *Tao Te Ching*, chapter 52.

brates at the same frequency. Fear pulls fear, anger pulls anger, and love pulls love.

Taoists believe that, as far as karma is concerned, when you acknowledge and accept your self and your reality, you need not have concern for past karma, unless there are other unusual circumstances (like past life experiences). Only the virtue you practice in the present is important, because Taoists believe that most karma is immediate.

The subtle Law of Energy Response represents a networking of energy that extends around and throughout the universe, much like the meridians that extend around and throughout your body, or like the planetary meridians that extend around the Earth. This network of energy contains the galaxies, stars, and planets within its domain. Taoists relate to the subtle law of energy response as the energy of the Great Mother, or *Kan Ying*, which means essentially that for every action there is a response, in some ways similar to the Hindu and Buddhist concept of karma. Any movement generates a similar, if not a countermovement. As the universal energies interweave into a net that comprises the subtle energy network of the Great Mother, they act in accordance with Divine Law, to maintain the harmony and balance within the universe. This represents the function of the feminine principle, the law of nature or the law of non-infringement.

The Law of Energy Response is more aggressively responding to the imbalances on the Earth at this time. It is acting to rebalance the Earth and everything on it. Those who misuse the law of energy response find it is one with the law of non-infringement and responds accordingly. They attract to them the same quality of energy they give off. Exceptions to this might be the necessity for one to live through the karma of past lives, or living through a group karma experience. In periods like this, at the end of an age and the beginning of a new age where the key word is "transformation," the karmic lessons are always very intense. The end of an age resolves the obstructions and restrictions of old energies, and brings in a positive energy of new life and regeneration to revitalize the incoming age.

The working of this law represents the unfolding of the Divine Plan. It is the Will of the Creator. How this unfolds is flexible to a point, as we all have free will, but major karmic lessons will become manifest. How you live through them depends upon your own attitude and how you perceive the reality before you. If this reality is formed from the outside, without the balancing effects of the internal practices of meditation, prayer, and your own soul-searching to bring your internal life into balance with your external life changes, you will find imbalances within your reality that you will have great difficulty resolving.

As the universal energies interweave into a net comprising the subtle energy network of the Great Mother, they act as a subtle energy regulator. If you ignore the power of the subtle energy network, with energy too strong or too weak, you will not channel yourself sufficiently well into the normal flow of life. It is preferable, therefore, to act and react with purpose, but gently, as any aggressive action tends to bind you by the restrictions created by your own energy. It is advantageous to understand this law of energy response before you attempt to employ any kind of aggressive action. This law warns people of the danger of forcibly trying to obtain their own worldly desires. The extent of your spiritual protection is the result of your own action under the Universal Law, which is operating perpetually within the universal energy net.[7]

Since the subtle energy network and its gross material counterpart, with its seemingly destructive side, represent different aspects of the energy of the Great Mother, you can call on Her for protection to get through turbulent times. The Great Mother can help you be a surfer of life's waves.

When we restore the natural integration of the physical, emotional, and mental bodies, and balance the energies of yin and yang within ourselves, we become open to the spiritual energy of shen, or Spirit. As we integrate our

---

[7] Insights from the subtle law of energy response are drawn from Master Hua Ching Ni, trans., *Complete Works of Lao Tzu* (Santa Monica, CA: The Shrine of the Eternal Breath of Tao, 1979), pp. 148–151 and pp. 216–217.

lives with the positive powers of the deities, saints, or immortals through self-cultivation, we revitalize our health, prolong our lives, and are a help to all those connected to us.

Living in the way of the Tao is like taking a leap of faith and living creatively in the world around you in positive relationship with the Universal Law and the law of non-infringement. Nourished by the energy of the Great Mother and guided by the enlightened vision of your own higher self, you walk your own way through the darkness within darkness into the light.

6

Good and Evil;
Abundance
and Infringement

Good and evil owe their existence to the Universal Law
and the law of non-infringement. It is precisely because of
the working of these two laws that we have good and evil,
or metaphysically, destiny and fate. Destiny represents the
heights you can reach by living in harmony with the law.
Fate represents the backward-going spiral into which you
can slip when you live in ignorance of the law.[8]

Destiny represents your greatest good. It represents not
only a goal to achieve, but work to be done. In living to
fulfill your destiny, you overcome your fate. By introspec-

---

[8] Insights on destiny and fate inspired by Deng Ming Dao's *Seven
Bamboo Tablets*. (San Francisco: HarperCollins Publishers, 1986),
pp. 15–17.

tion, you can know your destiny. It begins to become clear through the inner voice of intuition. Through intuition, you come into attunement with, and stay in attunement with, higher self. It is through higher self that you know and work out your destiny.

Fate represents the consequences of your past actions, your unfulfilled karma. It represents the quality of your soul's nature, brought forth from the past. It represents your gifts and abilities, as well as the obstacles and obstructions in your life. These indicate areas you should work in and things you should work on. By doing that, you can clear the way to go within and discover that task that is your life's work, to achieve your destiny.

Fate presents the world as a maze or an enigma that you have to work your way through. To one without understanding, fate may appear as evil. Fate is neither good nor evil, fate just is. It is how you live through your fate that determines whether it is good or evil. If you pursue your destiny, you come closer to heaven. Yield to fate, and you slip toward hell. It has been said that heaven and hell are right here on Earth. So don't look outside yourself for heavenly beings and hellish demons. Look within.

You must understand that your actions alone move you toward your destiny, or allow you to be overcome by your fate. Nothing else is involved. Diligently and creatively work out your fate and you will see your destiny unfolding before you. Give in to fate and your way becomes obscured.

In early shamanic religious traditions, all creation was imbued with spirit. All things were considered to be of divine origin. People not only showed respect for the divine forces of the heavenly realm, but for the divine forces of the earthly realm as well. Earth Mother, with all her creatures and things, was considered sacred. With this understanding, you can see that it would be impossible to live without infringing on something else. Every action, therefore, has some consequence or infringement. In this light, the law of non-infringement and the law of karma come together as one and the same law. Although it is almost impossible to live in the world without infringing on someone or something, you can work to fulfill your destiny, while trying not to create unnecessary consequences.

Retribution only exists within the mechanism of consequence. The mechanism of consequence is the subtle law of energy response, or the functioning of the law of non-infringement. Unless you aggressively seek to work out your destiny yourself, the law of non-infringement or the law of karma will do it for you. That is the working of fate. So there is such a thing as divine retribution. It is punishment neither decreed by God, nor by the Devil. Divine retribution is the interaction between destiny, fate, and consequence. That is all.

7

Tint To:
The Universal Law
(Continued)

The Universal Law of Abundance works with us because, we are seeing a part of ourselves, and we are simply opening up to a part of ourselves. That's really all it is. Abundance is being open to everything around you, and knowing that everything around you is a manifestation of what you are—the God force, the Tao within all things. Everything, in essence, is following this cycle of evolution. It is a perception of the fact that everything you see outside yourself is really a part of you. If it is a part of you, then you are already connected to it, and that connection allows you to be a part of all things. The way to do it is first to identify with it; but that's the hardest thing to do—identifying with the God force, the Tao.

Usually self-worth is our criterion for identifying. It is also, therefore, our stumbling block. Most of us feel we are not worthy of being the Tao, that we cannot be this magnanimous energy. Why? Because there are so many things we've done in our lives, so many things we still have to live through, that we feel we are not in control. This is the separation we feel between the Tao and ourselves. The only way to get the control is to realize your self-worth and identify with the Tao.

When you identify with the things around you, they basically become a conveyance of you. Anyone who has plants or animals knows they react to you. Even if you have a household of ten people, the dog knows who the master is. The dog knows the person with whom their energy can interact. You raise plants and give them much love and care. When you go on vacation, a friend waters the plants while you are gone. When you return, you wonder what your friend could have been putting on your plants. That projection signifies your relationship to your plants. Everything with which you interact becomes a part of your life and makes your life meaningful. Animals can make your life meaningful. Plants can make your life meaningful. Likewise, the things you wear can make your life meaningful. They give off an energy, a conveyance of you. Other people may not see it, but to you they have meaning or you would not be wearing them. If you wear them and you feel lousy, something is wrong. You have to free yourself of that wrong identification. Everything that's around you conveys a livingness in you. They don't necessarily make your life complete, but they allow you to be you. That's the whole idea: they allow you to be what you are.

If you find that you have things that are not you, pass them along. Let them go. By letting go, you feel more complete and this allows the opening for abundance to manifest. In a sense, you begin to feel more abundant as you begin to understand this concept of abundance. Remember, a part of wisdom is knowing that you have to stop trying to make objects or people into what they are not. You have to let them be what they are. If you understand yourself, you have to let yourself be what you are. If you are what you are, then how can other people, affect what you are?

At the same time, abundance is not infringement. Basically, every object, plant, or animal in this world is a vibration that is contained within humankind. We are basically the highest combination of all vibrations within the physical dimension. If you are a combination of the mineral, plant, and animal kingdoms, you can pull anything within those kingdoms to you, because they are a part of you. But, as I have said, you are the Tao, so if you try to pull another individual to you, you have two Tao forces working on each other. If your vibrations are higher, it will be easier for you to pull that person to you, but that becomes infringement. Why? Because you are trying to get something by interfering with someone else. However, when this happens naturally and spontaneously, it is because both individuals are vibrating in tune with each other.

If you let someone else's inability to feel good make you feel bad, you get into situations that prevent you from expressing the Tao within you. If you feel bad about yourself because someone else feels bad about him- or herself, you become heavily involved in emotions. If you let what other people say arouse you physically, emotionally, or intellectually, you become enmeshed in things that literally pull you back to the physical. Abundance does not allow you to control other people. It doesn't work that way. You can not demand, you can only attract things that vibrate at the same frequency. If you attract things that simply do not belong, or that do not make your life complete, you are attracting the wrong things. There should be a consistency of energy. The vibration constantly tries to maintain that consistency.

That is what we mean when we say that enlightenment is a type of vibrational energy. When you reach a certain vibration, you feel in tune with the world. That vibration is constantly being pulled back, however, as it is also being pulled forward. So you have to maintain it. Enlightenment does not involve reaching a certain point and that's it; it continues on, and on, and on. Neither does enlightenment mean that you are somewhere beyond human beings. It simply means you are being human. That's what enlightenment is all about. You simply are being what you are, and that is what you are. It's inside you already; you don't have to go anywhere to look for it. You have to let it come out of yourself. There has to be a consistency, a feeling of abundance that allows the energy to go into the situation, because you are already a part of the situation. There is no waiting. You must say, "I need something," not "Well, let me patiently sit and wait for this." There is no waiting involved. That's why the Universal Law is different from wishing and praying for something, and waiting for it to come. There is no waiting because you and the thing are already one. It's a process of alignment.

As you begin to understand your relationship to the world, first on the physical, then on the emotional, intellectual, and finally the spiritual world of abundance, you literally become open to the greater part of what you are, your higher self. That's what we mean when we say that you must see the inner beauty of you, to see yourself as beautiful, to see yourself as having inner worth. Spiritual energy can take whatever energy it needs to grow and complete itself. When you start to understand, you begin to disengage yourself from the world. That's when you reach a point where you know you can be everything.

This means that you literally begin to disengage from the physical, because you are already everything there is in the physical. As you detach yourself from the world and the people in it, you realize that all is well in the world, that everything in the world is happening the way it should, because it's carrying out the cycle of evolution.

You know, first of all, about yourself, and when you are satisfied with yourself, you enter a point of equilibrium, a point of balance. There is no bad, there is no good here, but it's not a point of apathy. There are no word games involved. You can be this; you can be that; because everything is in relation to everything else. Nothing is long and nothing is short, it's just relative to everything else, and that makes it what it is. As you disengage from the world, if you hear someone say, "this thing is terrible," you realize this thing isn't really terrible. It's only the other person's mind that says it's terrible. It's their perception that makes it terrible, and that perception is relative to them. It's also relative to your truth, to your beliefs, and if you believe you are all things, then everything is the way it is, because you are all things, and you are following evolution.

This is very hard to understand, because we want to quantify, we want to isolate, we want to be able to put this here and put that there. Why? It makes us comfortable in our minds. We don't want our mind bogged down with everything in this world. It's very hard for our mind to focus on this world, so we quantify it, neatly putting it away. We think we know what it's all about. So these are all our relativities; these are all the things we have put away, that have become our truths. They become our perception of what the world is.

At this point, you judge nothing, because there is nothing to judge. There is nothing good to judge, there is nothing bad to judge. There is no relativity other than your own reality with which you are working. If someone comes up to you and says, "today was a terrible day." It doesn't really give you a chance to have your own opinion, does it? It hardly gives you a chance to say, "Well, I actually like it when it rains." You cannot let other people decide your reality for you. You cannot let other people place their reality on yours. You have to be comfortable with what you are, and by being comfortable with what you are, you begin to identify with what you are. It may seem as if you are kind of going back and forth, but that's the whole idea. Identification is always the hardest thing to resolve—knowing who you are, identifying with what you are, and knowing you are the Tao.

When you stop quantifying the world, when you stop isolating the world and trying to give it your relativity, you become open to a very great secret. You begin to understand and experience the world as a feeling, and no longer as a decision. That's a very great secret, because since we don't have to decide anymore, we don't have to judge. When someone walks up to you and says, "What do you do?" And you say, "Nothing," then they are puzzled, because they don't know how to make an assessment of you. When you tell them what you do, that's how they can measure you. That's how they can tell who you are and what you are, based on their reality. However, if you say, "I do nothing," they don't know how to measure you. Most of the time, people assess you based on your actions, your dress and manner, on what you do outside of yourself. It is the same thing with your vibrations, it is something they perceive from the energy emanating from you. That's how they perceive you, but that, in essence, is not really you. It's not the vibrations that count, but the energy you have to understand.

This is when you can begin to live life and stop judging it. You will have no need to say, "Well, yesterday was a pretty good day; today was a lousy day, until five o'clock came." You no longer need to judge; you no longer have to make that point of reference. There is no frame of reference when you get to this place. There are no parameters on which you have to rely, no definitions that you need to determine who you are, because you simply know who you are. When you experience it, you don't have to quantify it. You do not have to say, "I like it;" you do not have to say, "I dislike it." This gives you an infinity of expressions, because you no longer allow quantification. I you an infinite range of expression, because you can ex press it as much as you want, as good as you want, as bad as you want, in as many different ways as you want, be cause you never gave it a definition. It becomes an experi ence that can become total, in terms of what you are do ing, because you are starting to feel the energy.

When you quantify, you find there are limitations. When you stop quantifying, you find there are no limita tions. That is another realization, that you are indeed this thing we call the Tao. The moment you say, "My life is this," it becomes what you say it has become. Now you have to think about what your life is. Now you have to begin to work on yourself. Once you become uninvolved with the world, once you begin to disengage from it, you don't quantify, you don't describe yourself. Why? This would lead you back into the same thing again, defini tions and limitations. That's what you're doing when you define yourself. By learning to go within your self, you learn to center your mind. Centering on this Universal Law is what is meant by discipline. Discipline is a center ing of self. It is indeed a turning in to your self, an iden tification of your self, and a knowing that it is your self rules your life.

True Mind means true identification. The initiate un derstands the negativity that exists within this world. The initiate also understands that this negativity is created by the mind, our perception of what is going on in the world. Even if you become enlightened, even if you become an initiate, there's still that little tiny amount of negativity that can grab you and pull you back. So you should always try to maintain this idea of abundance. You never reach a point where you can say, "I'm totally abundant." Rather, you are always trying to maintain total abundance. It's not that you gain power and the game is over; it's about evolution. You are constantly affirming the Tao within yourself. You are constantly affirming the infinity that you have, and you are constantly maintaining it, always trying to maintain balance. Balance is not a static condition; it is something that's constantly trying to maintain itself. If you allow the world to pull you back because you are not in positive relationship to it, then you are not being yourself. Remember, everything that is pulled to you is pulled to you because of you. At the same time, you are being pulled to the thing. It involves a connection between subject and object, but you cannot conceptualize it. If you try to explain this whole theory in reality, it won't work, for you cannot learn abundance. You can not learn how to be abundant. Your subconscious has to unlearn it. You have to unlearn your relativity to get back to the original point.

If you try to conceptualize abundance, you'll find it doesn't work. You cannot just say, "Hey, today I learned the Law of Abundance, and I learned how to live with it, and be in the magnificence of it." You have to live it; you have to be a part of it. Learning to live in accordance with the Universal Law requires that you develop discipline.

Discipline is actually when the Universal Law is working within your self. It is the discipline of self. You deal with your life and the things of everyday life; you deal with who you are, and with the concept of beginning to be. Simply be who you are. If you feel that at some point in the future, you will be complete, that you are not complete now, that means you are hampering the energy, you are bringing it down. You are hampering your discipline of self. You are telling your energy that you are not ready to be you.

When people say to you, "Hey, you know, you are getting older," it may mean they think you have less energy, or that you are not capable of becoming more of your self, or that, as you get older, you become less and less. That's the kind of thing that destroys the concept of the Tao. As you get older, you actually become more in tune with the energy, so you should be more of the Tao.

Those who say they are getting older, or somehow imply that they are getting weaker because they are getting older, are killing themselves. They are literally telling the Tao, "I'm getting older, so I cannot be as strong." Even though they say the Tao is all things, because they tend to take the Tao physically, emotionally, and mentally, they, out of habit, relate to it as a physical, emotional, and mental process. So, if you think you are getting older, you are not. You are only getting stronger with the Tao, if you can tune into it.

Living by the Universal Law is a discipline within itself that allows you to be all things. In this way, you have freedom in your life. If you have discipline in all things through the Universal Law, then you are totally free to be all you can be. By experiencing the Universal Law in your life, you become the observer. You no longer criticize or judge; you see the world for what it is. By using the Universal Law, those things that you think you need no longer are needs, because they have already become a part of you. You become a part of them and you discover what the Taoists call True Tao, Ching To.

Ching To means "True You," and the Tao is really the way to understand ourselves. The Universal Law is a tool to understand your self. When you get to that point, there is no waiting, because it's not about being patient; it doesn't work that way. It's a process of growing. Even as you are reading about the philosophy, you are growing, because there is a connection between us. What is being said, you are saying within yourself. You may not be saying it in the same way, but however you say it, it is the moment that counts. The moment prevails, and truly allows you to be what you are. You have to care about who you are and what you are. The Tao certainly doesn't care about who you are until you care, first. That's the way it works. You have to care who you are, before everything around you cares who you are. It's important to understand that everything is living, that there is a livingness in all things. Then you come to the realization that everything has a life force. The chair you are sitting on has a life force; your tape recorder has a life force; your computer has a life force; and everything in this world has life force. Everything, fundamentally, is one and the same thing, subject and object.

If you say, "I do not have the time," you are stopping the flow. It's not other people who are stopping your flow, you are stopping your own flow. If you say, "I do not have the money," you are stopping your own flow. If you feel weak, you are stopping your own flow. If you feel disease, you are stopping your own flow. You have to tune into health; you have to tune into abundance. Everything is a state of being. Remember, health is not good or bad, it is a state of being that allows your self to be what you want your self to be. If you feel weak, if you feel disease, it's because you have allowed your self to be these things. Now, if you don't like it, you can change it. When you wear a lot of clothes you don't like and you feel lousy about it, you have to do something about it. Only in that way will you begin to identify with what you are. Remember it's all energy, and energy can never be confined. Although you may think of energy as confined to the light bulb, it's not confined to the light bulb. It's flowing through the light bulb. Energy can never be confined. If it can never be confined, you must let it circulate. You must also let abundance circulate, for yourself and everyone around you.

You can have abundance, but are you ready to share it? If you are not, the Universal Law of Abundance won't work for you. You cannot restrict the Universal Law of Abundance to yourself; that means you don't see it as all things. If you see yourself as wealthy, everything around you becomes wealthy. If you see yourself as healthy, those things that are a greater part of your life become healthy. This discipline has to be a dedication. This dedication has to be a discipline.

All this discipline or dedication really involves is that you know that what you were is now no longer. Your realities prior to this moment are no longer relevant. What you are at this moment is what is important. It is always now that is important. The future is now, because the future comes from the present. The more you are now, the more you become in the future. If you already believe it, it will already be in the next moment. If you are healthy in this moment, you will be healthy in the next moment. If you feel disease and you say, "Health is something I have to achieve," then you may have a long way to go, but if there is disease, and you feel healthy now, then you are healthy now. You will begin to perceive it as you begin to become involved with the actual feeling of health. So discipline is, something like a "now-ism." You have to deal with now, because now is where the energy is. Energy is constantly changing, but it's changing now, not in the past or in the future. It's changing now. If you feel it and it's there, it materializes. But if you try to understand how this whole thing works, or how you can ever understand abundance, or how you can understand the Tao, it doesn't work. Why? The mere fact that you try to understand it, that you try to define it, prevents it from taking place, because the mind gets in the way.

When you ask how or why it can be done, what you are really asking is the question of order, reason, and doubt. When you ask how, you are questioning the order that transition goes through in becoming. When you ask, "Why?" you are asking for a reason why this can be done, but you also imply the question, "Can it be done?" So you acknowledge there is a doubt within it. And when you have doubts within yourself, the Tao simply cannot come true. If you ask how you are going to do this, no one can tell you how or why. Only you yourself can perceive how from within, through your contemplation on the basic framework of the Way of the Tao.

Now you are getting to the place that has no frame-work, and you might therefore say, "This seems easy. Show me how to do it." If you cannot come into the Tao without being told how to do it, it cannot be done. You must act on what you believe, on your highest perceptions of what is true for you. When you ask, "How?" the only answer is, "It's natural." How can anyone explain that? It's natural; it's spontaneous. There is no thought to it. It is happening in the moment.

Truth is basically a freezing of life. When you say something is true, you freeze life. It is true at the moment, because we are concerned with what is true in our lives at this particular moment. That's the reason why we hold onto everything that makes our lives meaningful, and the things that are true make our lives meaningful. Why? Because we are not seeing ourselves as eternal.

If you saw yourself as eternal, would you want to hold onto the truth? Truth that is experienced in relativity, now, would not necessarily be truth later. So you do not care about the truth anymore, you only care about the progression. You only care about eternity. That's when you realize that you are no longer separate. You only feel separate when you have to worry about next week. And when you worry about next week, you lose the moment of now. If you understand that you are eternal, you do not have to hold onto something, you do not have to defend it, you do not have to protect it. You only have to protect it if you really believe it's true, but it's only true within the moment. The next moment, it may be something else. You must feel your eternity, feel your abundance, and then you will be able to tune into the abundance that you are. If you feel there is something missing in your life, acknowledge it to exist in your life, and it will be pulled into your life. Don't acknowledge it as an ultimate goal or something that you seek, because the mere fact that you seek ensures that you will not find. That's the paradox of the Tao. In the way of the Tao, everything is paradoxical. What is, isn't; and what isn't, is. What is good is bad, and what is bad is good. In life, everything is always perceived within a framework of relativity. When we transcend relativity, we go into what we call the Universal Law of Abundance and evolution. For, although we are living in this time and space, when we reach the inner core of ourselves, we transcend time and space. Why? Because we become evolution. Evolution is time and space, so we become all that there is to become.

PART 2

Te—Virtue (Integrity)

When the superior man hears the Way,
   He is scarcely able to put it into practice.
When the middling man hears the Way,
   He appears now to preserve it, now to lose it.
When the inferior man hears the Way,
He laughs at it loudly,
   If he did not laugh,
      It would not be fit to be the Way.
For this reason,
There is a series of epigrams that says:
   "The bright Way seems dim.
   The forward Way seems backward.
   The level Way seems bumpy.
   Superior integrity seems like a valley.
The greatest whiteness seems like grime.
Ample integrity seems insufficient.

Robust integrity seems apathetic.
Plain truth seems sullied.

The great square has no corners.
The vessel is never completed.
The great note sounds muted.
The great image has no form.

The Way is concealed and has no name.
Indeed,
The Way alone is good at beginning
And good at completing.
—*Tao Te Ching*[9]

[9] Victor H. Mair, *Tao Te Ching* (New York: Random House, 1990), p. 7.

8

Negativity and Your Reality

There is no method or way to deal with negativity. It is something that you have to resolve within yourself. The only method you can rely on is rooted in how you deal with your life. Instead of talking about negativity, therefore, we'll talk about your reality. If your reality is negative, you will have to deal with negativity in your life. There is no one reality in our world; there is no one truth in our world. The only reality, the only truth, is that which you create within yourself. There is no absolute truth within this dimension that you can see or relate to outside of yourself. The truth is that which you have created within yourself. Reality is within you. If there is negativity in your life, understand that you have pulled it to you. If you say it belongs to someone else, that gives someone else power over you and your life. Accept your part of it—the hurt feelings and the negative emotions—and forgive. By forgiving someone else, and forgiving yourself, you take back your power. Stop using your personal power; it always brings unpleasant reactions. Using personal power imposes your will on someone else, which brings about conflict. Instead of trying to change someone else, change yourself.

Understand that all life is vibration, and you merge with what you relate or vibrate to. If you vibrate to anger, resentment, injustice, or self-pity, you will find these in your life at every turn. To change your life or your reality, you must change your vibration, or what you vibrate to. Take full responsibility for yourself, for your life, and for what you think, say, and do. Remember, the law of non-infringement represents that aspect of the Tao that brings to you the reactions to your past actions—those things we say and do to one another that come back to us with love, as the Great Mother's grace, to teach us how to love. Understand that you are of the Tao, and acknowledge its presence in your being and in your life. Come in tune with it by living in the light and using positive affirmations, mantras, meditation, and prayer. As you change, the conditions around you will change, and people will change. When you are undisturbed by these situations, they fall away of their own accord. Your life is a reflection of the sum total of your subconscious beliefs. Wherever you go, you take these conditions with you. Change your reality by changing yourself and the way you relate to people and the world around you, and negativity will just fall away.

9

Reality

In order to understand the Mystery of reality, we need
   not only
reflection or thought but vision - the vision of the
   whole.
This, however is not possible without imagination,
the ability to re-create reality in the image of our deepest experience.
Without the creative faculty our mind is only a
weak reflection of fleeting sense impressions.
Creative imagination is the motor, the moving power,
reason the steering and the restricting faculty
which distinguishes between the potential and the actual,
the probable and the possible.

        —The Inner Structure of the I Ching[10]

---

[10] Lama Anagarika Govinda, *The Inner Structure of the I Ching* (Trumbull, CT: Weatherhill, 1981), p. 39.

In examining reality from a Taoist perspective, we find that none of the masters that have gone before have said there is one reality or only one truth. Even though there are people who say there is an absolute or an ultimate truth, no master has said that. People have translated the Tao as "the absolute." People have translated the Buddha as "the absolute," or God as "the absolute," but there really isn't any absolute truth outside yourself. There is only the truth within yourself. However, because we all see the world very differently, we all have very different definitions of the world in which we live. We all have very different definitions for what we perceive as truth, as reality. As time progresses, our reality begins to change. It may not be the same reality three minutes from now, a week from now, a month from now. It is like asking the question, "What is love?" Everyone can define what love is to a certain degree, but we cannot pinpoint it, or give an absolute definition. It's the same with reality; we can not give an absolute definition for that, either. The only definition you can give is what's true for you—what love means to you, what reality means to you.

The Four Aspects of Understanding Reality

In order to understand what reality is, we need to explore and understand the following four aspects:

1. You are the Tao.
2. The Four Steps.
3. Respecting evolution.
4. Stepping above free will into free flow.

You Are the Tao

The first and most important of the four aspects is "you are the Tao." To realize that you are the Tao, you must begin by loving yourself. Know you are the Tao, and know that the Tao is unconditional love. It has no conditions, no beginning, and no end. There never was a beginning and there never will be an end. You may say there is a separation from one world to another, from one essence to another, but that's evolution. That is not the end of something but rather something evolving from one aspect of being into another. In life, there is no end and there is no beginning. There is only livingness. When you recognize that you are the Tao, you realize the livingness in life.

The Tao is divine energy that permeates all existence. It is formless, but it animates all forms. Divine energy can adopt any form and manifest as deity for the benefit of worshippers. This is the cornerstone of devotional life, to give you a taste of the divine. Once you recognize that the divine is the energy generated during worship, that it is inside your own consciousness and being, your worship turns inward. Through the study of spiritual books and such, you can grow mentally, and can even become enlightened. You develop a spiritual mentality, and can give elaborate discourses on spirituality. But this is a realization of consciousness. Spirituality is the recognition that you are spiritual energy, that you are of the Tao; and that is a realization of being.

Spiritual development comes from being able to perceive internal energy. It's the recognition that you are spiritual energy, that you are the Tao. Then you begin to attune to immortality, to universality, to the eternity that's within. You won't be someone trying to be someone, you'll simply be. There is no longer that process of trying to be. You have always been the Tao, and you will always be the Tao. So you have to begin by loving yourself, you have to begin by recognizing that you are the Tao. And that is not an easy task, because it's not easy to look within yourself. Where do you begin? Should you begin with your body? Should you begin with your mind? Begin with the things that mean the most to you. How you perceive yourself is where you begin.

The Four Steps—Four Disciplines of Self

The second aspect of understanding reality is The Four Steps or Four Disciplines of Self. These steps are:

- physical discipline;
- mental discipline;
- discipline of harmony;
- discipline of balance.

Physical Discipline

Physical discipline is working on the body, with the body, and through the body. First you work on the body, and you begin to understand more about it. Then, you gain the facility to work with the body. You know the balances and the imbalances, and you work with them. When you establish that balance within imbalance, you can work through the body. In the practice of Tai Chi Chuan or Chi Kung, you first learn to begin working on the body. Once you begin to gain an awareness of the body, you begin to work with it. You know your body has a certain amount of strength, a certain amount of weakness. You begin to work with the abilities you have within the body, then you find you can work through it. In the last stage, the body becomes a vehicle of expression—an instrument, a vessel—which allows you to convey energy. In Tai Chi Chuan, this energy is called chi. Physical discipline means you begin to utilize your body to convey the Tao within you. Your body literally becomes a church, a temple of the Tao; it becomes a vehicle, the instrument that you use to convey the Tao within you.

Mental Discipline

Mental discipline is dealing with our perception of the world and how we relate to it. Whether we are healthy or diseased depends, to some degree, on the environment in which we live. Most of you know that we interact emotionally, and we can develop emotional imbalances that can cause disease. Mental discipline involves using your body and mind to relate to your environment and the people around you. If your body is in pain, if it develops some type of physical, mental, or emotional imbalance, there may be something faulty in the way you perceive and relate to yourself, to the world, or to those around you. How do you perceive yourself? What is your perception of the environment of which you are a part? Is it harmonious?

To achieve mental discipline, you must have mental clearing. Mental clearing is a tool that helps you become sensitized to the world around you and it helps initiate you into the Tao. It consists of four stages:

Self-examination and Forgiveness;
Understanding desires;
Recognizing infinity;
Affirming cause and effect.

Self Examination: Self-examination occurs when you begin to look at all parts of your life, when you look at every aspect of the things that influence your life, especially the negative ones. Are these the things that give your body discomfort, that give your body a sense of imbalance? Maybe you feel uncomfortable about your body; maybe you feel uncomfortable about your emotions. Begin to examine all these things. Why is it you are angry? Why is it you are jealous? Why is it you feel resentment? You begin to look at all of these things that make you hold on to a painful situation. When you get angry, you are holding on to something. When you are jealous, you are holding on to something. When you feel resentment, you are holding on to something. All of these things that make you hold on to something are causing your life to stagnate. They must become a part of the process of self-examination. One of the greatest spiritual processes, one of the greatest spiritual tools that comes from self-examination is forgiveness. But forgiveness has to be complete and thorough. When you look at yourself, and you begin to realize the imbalances that you have in your life, you begin to release them. You begin to forgive imbalances. Remember, forgiveness is not an energy that affects just you. It is an energy that affects you first, and then all those around you. Initiates know who they are and what they are, because they have released everything. That is the only way you can become an initiate. The only way you can start all over again is by releasing everything. Through self-examination of your emotions, you learn why you are. By self-forgiveness, you are able to let go of why you are and begin to know who you are. When you begin to work on emotions, you begin to understand your desires.

Understanding Desires: The second part of mental clearing is understanding desires, which deals with understanding your emotions. Desires are not bad; desires are not good. They are but an aspect of yourself that let you understand more about yourself. When you desire something, you have a chance to understand a little more about yourself, about what you need and what you don't need. Desires come from looking outside of yourself. However, it is when you begin to look outside of yourself that you begin to develop feelings of guilt and sin. Desires are not sin, because they do not separate you from the Tao. It is you yourself. Desires are your wishes to obtain something outside of yourself. Desires are physical, but they can be emotional or mental as well. In any case, desires mean we are attached to something. They constitute a tremendous force, and must be controlled and directed into the right channels. When you feel guilty or sinful, it is because you are ashamed to face yourself. That is an extension of self-examination. You have to release that guilt or sin. You have to forgive and seek forgiveness where necessary. Then you have to release it, you have to let go. You are really hurting yourself by not forgiving. When you begin to feel the excitement, the feeling involved in the process of forgiveness, you expose your emotions. You begin to realize why certain emotions are the way they are. Emotions are the way you perceive other people, and the way you perceive yourself. They really tell you why you live your life as you do, but they don't tell you who you are. Your emotions convey why you are, and why you react the way you do. This brings you to the third part of mental clearing, recognizing infinity.

Recognizing Infinity: To recognize infinity is to recognize that the Tao is everywhere and in everything. When you recognize infinity, your consciousness opens up to the Tao as higher self within. Living by the guidance of intuition from higher self purifies your consciousness and transforms your vital energy sufficiently to become open to Tai Chi, the subtle realm. To do this, Taoists use the magic circle to harmonize the eight subtle energies of the Pa Qua (see figure 2, page 11). When the finite mind reaches the point of infinity, it allows you to go beyond the finite. By your very presence, all those around you are helped, consciously or unconsciously, by the quality of your energy. By helping yourself to grow spiritually, you begin to help all those around you. By loving yourself, you begin to love the person next to you. There may be some people you dislike, but you can still love them. This brings us to the fourth stage of mental clearing—affirming cause and effect.

Affirming Cause and Effect: The fourth stage of mental clearing involves affirming the concept of cause and effect. You probably know it as karma. When you transcend cause and effect, you begin to realize that you have your own reality, and that no one else can say your reality is wrong. Regardless of what other people say about it, it's still your reality. Karma enables you to understand your reality. It allows you to understand evolution, to understand that you are the medium for karma. Karma exists because of you. If there weren't a "you," how could there be a cause, how could there be an effect? In essence, you are the medium that allows this thing we call karmic alignment to take place. Karma allows you to be fully you, so to speak. You do not receive something because you deserve it or because you are worthy of it. You receive it because it is already a part of you. That is a very important thing to understand about karma.

Some people feel they are poor because, in a previous life they did many bad things and now they have to suffer. Most karma, however, is immediate. It's based on what you do now, at this second, at this minute. If you feel that you are poor, then you have already created karma. You have already created the cause and the effect. If you acknowledge the fact that you are rich, however, you allow yourself to be the medium for richness to flow into your life. The highest expression of acknowledging that you are a medium is a prayer. A prayer is instantaneous and spontaneous. When you pray, you affirm that which you already are. If you feel that the opposite exists, and you wish that it didn't, you have already denied a struggle within yourself. To affirm Tao in your life, you must call on your higher self and speak in that consciousness and being, as though you two are one.

Discipline of Harmony

Many spiritual people have a lot of trouble achieving harmony. They live in the world, and see the good and the bad, and experience the pleasure and the pain. They try not to get too caught up in life's pleasures so they won't have to endure life's pains. Because of this, however, they never really live up to their full potential, and never fully realize the livingness of life. They see the yin and the yang, and they try to follow the middle path. That is the way of harmony: seeing both sides of the road, seeing the negative and the positive, the bad and the good. You see the way of the sinner and the way of the saint. You try to maintain harmony between the two. That is very difficult, because you try to maintain harmony through your own inner strength. You try to offset the negative by not accepting it or rejecting it. In a sense, you try to fight fire with fire. If someone throws something at you, do you throw something back? If you do, that is not a very harmonious situation. If someone throws something at you, don't return it—no matter whether it's thoughts, or a feeling, or an object, or energy. Why is that important? When you begin to develop harmony in your life, you begin to acknowledge that whatever is happening to you is happening because of you. If someone throws something at you, it is because it is you. They are throwing it at you because it has become a part of your reality. If you fight it, you are denying your reality. Your reality keeps you from becoming open to their reality. That's what causes the disharmonious situation. Harmony is within you. It's how you perceive yourself. It is a perspective, a conveyance of you. Walking in the middle is very difficult, because, when you walk in the middle, both sides hit you. If both sides hit you and you are not able to withstand that, you become disharmonious. However, if you are able to walk in the middle and maintain harmony, then you can begin to walk from side to side, and that's called balance.

Discipline of Balance

Balance vibrates at a much higher frequency then harmony, because it's a higher level of awareness. Everything is balance; everything is positive and negative; everything has two sides. You can choose to walk right in the middle, so you can avoid the positive and negative, but then both sides bombard you at the same time. If you try to keep just to the positive, the negative will continually bombard you. Positive and negative are always fluctuating, going from one side to the other all the time. So there has to be a sense of balance within imbalance, and there has to be a sense of imbalance within balance. There has to be a sense of harmony within disharmony, and a sense of disharmony within harmony. Being open to both sides, you come into balance. Balance is being able to go from one side to the other and not be affected by either. Balance means that you do not deny the other side. People think that to be spiritual, you have to deny the material realm, because materialism defies the spiritual. That's not true. The material and spiritual are both halves of the same thing; you go from one side to the other. So balance means there is both, and because there is both, the only way to maintain balance is to go deep into your own self.

You have to begin by relaxing your body and allowing it to have an inner solitude, an inner tranquillity that lets you center yourself on something. You can center on your higher self, or you can focus on the golden white light of the Creator in the middle tan tien, or the heart center (see Appendix II, page 261). That will eventually open the heart chakra and the center, or thrusting channels. You can center your mind there. In meditating on your higher self there, you find the way and means to turn the energy of your reality from negative to positive. You begin to see from one side to the other. You begin to go from harmonious life situations to very balanced life situations.

In your spiritual life, you might ask, "Why are so many things happening to me?" As you become more spiritual, you will experience negativity more and more—or, at least, you will get glimpses of those things that come from the subconscious and bother you. This happens because you are beginning to see the world. As you become more spiritual, you begin to see more of the world. You begin to open the inner world of yourself to the outer world around you. You begin to turn your inside out. You are no longer fighting it, you begin to be the observer. If you try to fight a storm, you do not see the calmness that comes right after. If you stand back, then you see both. If you see the storm, and you only see the negativity coming, you forget about the calm that comes right after. This means you are still fighting it. This means you are only trying to stay in the middle. You haven't gone from one side to the other; you haven't maintained the balance. Spirituality is vibrating at a much higher frequency because you are allowing yourself to be more open. At the same time, because you are more open, you become more vulnerable, you become more exposed. That's the reason you experience more chaos within your life. It's because the whole picture is coming together, and because the whole picture is chaotic, it takes a long time to come together. The reason why you may want to run away from it is because you have it within yourself. If you want to be a part of the Tao, you have to be in it; you have to be a part of the process. As was said about the inner door, if you go in, you have to go in all the way. If you just open and close the door, you are just trying to maintain harmony and will never come into balance. Balance is achieved when you can live in the two realms at one and the same time.

Respecting Evolution—The Tao of Change

One of the fundamental teachings of the Tao is respecting evolution, respecting all things because they are alive. Taoists believe in working on themselves to transform reality, rather than trying to impose their will on reality. They look at the world and try to work in harmony with life's changes. They know Mother Nature teaches them how to evolve, because it is by Her law of non-infringement that they learn how to live in love. Although change is constant in nature, there is an unchanging principle underlying all change. All beings and things are endowed with spirit, the eternal reality behind all change. There is no more graphic example of this than the four seasons. In spring, seeds are planted and vegetation appears to come to life. In summer, everything is in full bloom. In fall, we harvest the crops of spring. In winter, snow falls on the land, and it seems that all vegetation has died away, only to blossom once again in spring. In the same way, we are born, go through childhood, maturity, old age, and what appears as death, which is but transition or birth into another dimension. For one who identifies with the evolution of all life and relates to the multiple dimensions of the universe in a direct way, the universe is real. Those who perceive the universe as outside of themselves, see the universe as unreal or not a part of their reality. Real or unreal, reality or illusion, are two halves of the same whole. So moving from free will to freely flowing with the currents of the universe is how you learn to apply the results of your contemplations. This gives you the opportunity to practice your spirituality by living your philosophy among worldly people who have no regard for things of the spirit. The Tao of change is lived in the world so that we may go through transformation into the Tao, now.

Stepping above Free Will into Free Flow

The fourth aspect of understanding reality is stepping above free will into free flow. Free will means simply having the ability to choose, but you still have to choose. Free flow means you don't choose, you just flow with it; there is no choice, no decision made.

Stepping above free will into free flow is a changing of thought patterns. You are beginning to experience a change of perspective in your reality. You see the relativity in the reality before you, the reality by which you have allowed yourself to become restricted. You understand that this universe is the realm of free will, where everyone is endowed with the potential to create his or her own reality. You also understand that part of the paradox of living in the realm of free will is that all things are allowed, even tyrannies. So it is also a free choice to have someone else create your reality for you.

As you begin to live according to your own inner guidance and your own daring, everything changes completely. For now you know you are meant to discover your reality from within and to direct your life in this way. This is really the Creator's gift of grace to you in the realm of free will. Now that you are conscious, there is no need to strive to become; just be, because there is no judgment here, there is no mind.

When you come to free flow, you have to ask yourself: "Am I ready to be natural? Am I ready to be spontaneous?" This is a very difficult and usually very crucial point in leaving the mind. Most of us are not really ready to take that step. Most of us have a tendency to want to hold onto a little bit of what we enjoy in life, not knowing that what we enjoy has allowed us to become attached to the relativity in our lives. Everything you enjoy in life is relative to you, so, as long as you are still you, you will still experience the enjoyment. When you reach no mind, your mind does not think about things, because they are not on your mind. Your mind does not think about things as good or bad, it thinks about things simply because it is. It's a natural flow going through you. This realization will dissipate your attachment to many things around you, and they will disappear from your reality.

The real question now is are you ready for your world, so to speak, to shatter in front of you? Your world has been created by the realities that, over the years, you have allowed to be placed around you. Most of us don't want to give up the reality we experience. In shattering our world, we, in essence, are shattering our minds, because our minds are our world. No mind no world. This means spontaneity: everything is happening because of the flow. We just flow with it. You are here simply because you are here.

10

*Relationships
and Your Reality*

Man takes part in the forms of Heaven and Earth.

By assimilating himself to Heaven and Earth,
he will not get into conflict with them. (True Mind)
He enjoys Heaven and Knows his destiny; (Right Identification)
therefore he is free from worry. (True Reason)
He is content with his situation (Right Involvement)
and genuine in his sympathy, (True Virtue)
and is honest in his compassion (Right Manifestation)
Therefore he is able to give love. (True Tao)
          —*The Inner Structure of the I Ching*[11]

---

[11] Lama Anagarika Govinda, *The Inner Structure of the I Ching*
(Trumbull, CT: Weatherhill, 1981), p. 39.

To some degree, everyone has a relationship with the divine, the higher self, the all-that-is, regardless of what that relationship is. The only way that you become spiritually developed is when that relationship becomes conscious and begins to constantly change, grow, and transform. This relationship is seated in spiritual understanding. It is your relationship to the reality that is now before you. Your relationship with the divine simply defines what your reality is at this particular moment. That reality can be one of acceptance of everything that happens to you and around you, with spiritual maturity, which graces the reality that is before you.

Spiritual Understanding and Your Reality

In considering your reality, you may decide to accept only that aspect of your reality that you perceive as good and deny the rest. If you do that, you create a very emotional reality, one that essentially judges things to be good or bad. This is moralistic. You have judged your reality to be only those things you like and have rejected those you don't like. Thus, you do not really embrace the whole reality that is before you.

When you do not fully accept the reality before you, you do not fully live life. You just live on the surface of life, never diving deeply into the depths of your emotions, into the fullness of your being. Some of us simply do not like the reality that is before us, so we deny it. "This cannot be me. This cannot happen to me." "I don't know why I'm in this world." "It simply is not me." Even this, however, is still a relationship, and one that does not make you less spiritual than someone who embraces all that is before them. When you find you have the power to change those aspects of your reality you cannot accept, and accept those aspects of your reality you cannot change, you are ready to move on. The only way you grow is by not getting stuck within the reality you are in, and constantly staying within that reality.

By the same token, to understand spirituality is to understand that spirituality is not a way, a path, a method, or a discipline. It is a state of being. You can go to classes for personal growth, and study psychology, to help better adapt yourself to deal with situations of life in the world. But spirituality is not a discipline to help you make yourself better. Spirituality doesn't make you better; it simply makes you more. It allows you to open to a level of consciousness and being that is much greater than what you now experience. It allows you to be more of yourself. Classes on spirituality can offer you a way, a technique, or a method, that will allow you to bring your consciousness and being into alignment with the spirit. This alignment can be in a very philosophical perspective, or it can be within a religious perspective. It can be in a healing perspective, or it can be in an active, creatively doing perspective. We try to use this alignment as a tool to get to spirit. But we shouldn't get caught up in a particular technique or alignment, or align ourselves to a reality that is outside ourselves.

When you walk the way of the Tao, you align yourself with certain concepts that exist within certain principles, or with a philosophy to which you have an affinity. You may like reading about it, or enjoy listening to it and experiencing it. But if you follow it in such a way that you see it as outside yourself, then what you are experiencing is not a manifestation of yourself, but an attempt to manifest something about which you have read, or an experience you are anticipating. However, what you are doing is following an alignment, trying to place someone else's reality on yourself. The problem that comes when we look outside of ourselves is that we can never get enough. We want more. We begin to depend upon inspiration from the outside. "Give me more information on the Tao. Give me more information about Buddha." We want to get as much information as possible about it because we have a tendency to look outside ourselves for everything. We then lose the essence of it, however, because we try to experience more of it outside of ourselves than we do within. Those who experience spiritual realization in this way develop their consciousness without necessarily transforming their being.

It is important to realize that the relationship is always from within yourself and how you perceive the world unfolding in front of you. These realizations of consciousness must be balanced or rooted within your realization of being, your true knowing—a gut feeling, an aliveness, a livingness opening in your heart. In the beginning, you may take to other disciplines or take on other alignments, because they give you a point of reference from which you can start. You can say, "I'm following the Taoist approach," or "I'm following the Buddhist approach," and so on. It helps you get your bearings as to "who I am", "where I'm coming from", and then, "where I'm going".

Spirituality is that spark of aliveness that links you, as soul, with spirit. It can be triggered from outside, but it always manifests from within. It represents the dimension Taoists call Tai Chi, in which one becomes open to transformation by spiritual energy. Tai Chi is the spiritual realm, the realm of the deities, Immortals, masters, and initiates.

In Tai Chi, spiritual understanding truly becomes your reality. When you become open to Tai Chi, you become an initiate, one who does not follow any other way except his or her own from higher intuition. Initiation means you follow your own path, fulfill your own destiny. When you create the reality, you know it is your own reality, from your own higher self. You are no longer a Taoist per se; you are no longer a Buddhist per se. You are you, and whatever is happening in front of you is your reality, because you initiate it, you create it. You no longer follow a path that's set before you. You create your destiny for yourself, no one else creates it for you. To do this is to find the beauty within your self. By embracing your self, by embracing your whole being, your higher and lower selves become one. You are now able to look at yourself and have a sense of acceptance of who and what you are.

The first question you should ask yourself is: "If I had the opportunity to be anyone in the world, who would I want to be?" Well, the answer has to be you. If it is not, you haven't begun to embrace yourself. You have not been willing to accept who you are. You want to follow someone else's destiny; you want to follow or use someone else's images and projections to create your own reality.

If you have embraced your self, but not fully, to that same degree, you have still embraced the reality that is before you; the rest is veiled in shadows.

The Way is not so much rejecting the so-called negativity that you experience, because a seemingly negative thing can happen to anyone. If you don't perceive a thing as negative, however, it cannot be negative. It's your perception and how you react to that perception that creates the positive and negative realities that befall you. If you perceive a seemingly negative thing in a positive way, you transform the nature of its energy. So negativity and positiveness, in essence, are very relative concepts. In Taoist terms, they are called yin and yang. They are really two parts of one whole thing; it's just that when you take one part of a whole thing and want to experience it, you automatically become aware of the opposite part. And that's the whole concept of the Way.

By trying to maintain harmony in your life, you travel the middle path and get hit by both sides. By maintaining balance, on the other hand, you can move from yin to yang, from one side to the other, without the need to judge. You can be open to both the positive and negative experiences within your reality. That reality is really a steppingstone to something else. As evolution itself is endless, consciousness is endless as well—it never stops. Even if you reach an enlightenment, it's always a stepping-stone to something else, for evolution never stops; it's constantly moving and evolving.

There is a story about Lao Tzu and Chuang Tzu, two much-beloved characters of the Taoist tradition. Lao Tzu was walking with Chuang Tzu along the road, followed by a disciple. They came upon a river, and Lao Tzu and Chuang Tzu walked across it. When the disciple saw the two masters walk across the river, he scratched his head and decided he was going to do the same thing. So he went to walk on the water and fell in. Lao Tzu and Chuang Tzu looked back and said, "Should we tell him where the stones are?"

The idea behind the story is that your reality is the reality that you see before you. It should not be a reality that you think is there, but one that you know is there. You cannot say, "I think I can walk on water." You have to have a knowing. You must constantly live through the reality that is before you. You can't be ambivalent about it, because if there is doubt, that means you have doubt about yourself. You have to fully embrace who you are.

Spiritual understanding essentially means that you begin to take responsibility for your life. And taking responsibility for your life means taking responsibility for your reality, for the things that are happening in front of you, in you, and around you. You become your own initiate, because that's the only way you can become very intimate with yourself. Intimacy only comes through an acceptance of self. How else can you know yourself, if you are not willing to embrace yourself? You may say, "I love myself, but what can be done about all the problems of the world?" If you really love yourself, you already know what can be done about the problems of the world, because the world becomes a manifestation of your love. Love is not an inward-going energy; it's an outward-going energy. It's always expansive. So it's out of love for yourself that you begin to understand the world.

First, however, you have to accept and love every aspect of yourself in order to become whole as soul. As your concept of self expands and becomes linked by intuition with higher self, your love of self expands. Expressed through higher self as deity or master, immortal or teacher, you become the initiate. You become open to the Divine Mother in many of Her aspects: as the Great Mother, Mother Nature, the Terrible Mother, the Holy Ghost, the feminine principle, creation, being, the Tao of yin. You also come to know the Divine Father in many of His aspects: creator, preserver, destroyer, Spirit, the masculine principle, Universal Mind, consciousness, the Tao of yang. You begin to gain spiritual understanding; you begin to understand why your reality is as it is. You learn how you can make internal changes in your consciousness and being to bring about external changes in your reality. Through positively transforming your reality, you become a conscious partner with the creator in the transformation of the reality before you.

The world you begin to understand becomes a very loving world, because its reality becomes a projection of who you are. Whoever you are, if you want to become spiritually involved, you have to do so by taking responsibility for your own self, by being willing to change. Your alignment has to be shattered. The only way it can be shattered is if you are willing to move beyond it, if you are willing to step above it, if you are able to transcend it, because everything is a stepping-stone to something else.

There is, however, something that always gets in the way—the ego. The ego is that aspect of yourself that thrives on security. It provides the security that makes your reality firm. Without the ego, your reality right now might be a little shaky. The ego creates the security that allows you to exist in the world without constant anxiety, without fear, or doubt. The ego, on the other hand, very often makes you a victim of the world you are in, rather than an initiate. By giving you security, it blames society. It heaps blame on society, on your partner, on your parents, on your friends and neighbors. That is how it allows you to maintain security, by allowing you to become a victim of the world around you. We do this all the time. When something terrible happens, we don't want to be the cause of the problem, we want to be its victim. We blame someone outside of ourselves.

It's very easy to look out and see the problems of the world, but it's very hard to find the problems within ourselves, to look deep within ourselves and understand these problems. The problem is everyone and everything except you—that's what the ego tells you. The ego tricks you. It says you are a beautiful person, and the world is a crummy place. So you become a victim of everything that's wrong—except yourself. Because of this, you have to learn how to tolerate and to suffer or endure. If, indeed, you are a beautiful person and everything else in the world is terrible, you have to learn how to suffer and endure, learn how to tolerate.

Spirituality is not, however, about tolerance. Spirituality is about transformation. It is about the way you can change the reality you have before you. It's not about looking at the world and seeing something terrible, of which you are a victim. Nor is it about tolerance. It's about creating a reality that is a manifestation of your self. If you want to be someone else, what you are really saying is that you don't want to deal with the intimacy of yourself. You don't want to get involved in the intricacies that are involved in taking the responsibility for creating your own reality. The price of identifying yourself with someone or something else is that you have to live up to the image of that identification. Whenever you identify with something outside you, you create and image of yourself —an image that you have to live up to. Remember, images precede reality. You have to have an image of something before it can become a reality. Conception precedes manifestation. You have to conceive of something before it can manifest. So if you have an image of what to identify with, you have to live up to that image. The image you have created and identified with becomes a projection outside of yourself. Every time you align with someone or something outside of yourself, you create your limitations, because alignment means it's properly defined. When something is properly defined, it cannot be something else. That means you have defined the limitations within the alignment. So by defining, you restrict the change, you restrict the choices. Spirituality, however, is not about restriction. It's about transformation, about constantly being able to transform.

The saddest part is when the reality you create through identifying and defining collapses—a reality that you have placed within yourself from something outside of yourself—you begin to worry, you feel guilt, and become depressed. All of these things, in one way or another, are different forms of anger. Chinese medicine teaches that anger restricts movement. It creates what is called "reckless chi." That means that the energy in the body goes haywire; it goes anywhere it wants. Your body loses control; the energy doesn't know where to go. This loss of control makes you unable to move, unable to be spontaneous, unable to move in the flow of your creation. Because of this, many classes in spiritual understanding are, in essence, really classes in psychological growth, to get you to the point where you can go beyond the worry, guilt and depression.

So why suffer? That's really the question. If you follow the Universal Law of Abundance, aware that the world is a world of abundance, then why must you suffer? There is a choice you can make spiritually. There are alternatives; there are different ways that you can grow spiritually, without suffering, without agony. If you think that to grow spiritually, you have to experience pain, that's only a reality that you have allowed to become a part of your world. If you think that is the only way, you have taken a very narrow view of spiritual understanding. You do not need to experience pain to understand joy.

When you begin to create your own reality, pain and suffering become opportunities for you to grow and go beyond your present reality. Spiritual understanding is not just an intellectual understanding, but a transformation in your being or feeling nature. Through transformation, you become open to the spiritual realm, and can experience joy without necessarily going through the suffering and agony that is very often called part of spiritual understanding. You become happier, more in control of your life. You are no longer a victim of your own life. In essence, you learn to love yourself, and to love life. Spiritual understanding is, ultimately, an understanding of love and what it means to love.

So it is said that it is not your actions that make you; it is your reactions. If you react positively to all of life's situations, understanding that the divine is in all life, this brings about the transformation of energy that allows you to endure. You don't have to seek joy, because the nature of spiritual energy is joyous and transforming. This is not, however, something that will automatically embrace you, help you, or work with you. Rather, it is an alternative that you can embrace and work with when you take responsibility of your own life. You create the reality before you. The joy and happiness is there, provided you are willing to accept the world. Spirituality doesn't mean you have to save the world. The world is fine the way it is. But evolution never stops; you just have to move within its flow.

Self-Forgiveness

Self-Forgiveness is a process, and self-love is a process. They are intertwined. Not forgiving is self-pity. You only know it as self-pity because other people see it and begin to feel sorry for you. If you get the help you seek, you will seek it again in a similar situation, thus never getting beyond your present hang-up. Remember, self-examination and forgiveness are the first steps to mental clearing.

The process of self-forgiveness consists of four steps: working on the emotional body; working on the mental body; working on the physical body; and working with the spiritual body. I describe these steps in this sequence for presentation only; you can live through this process in any order.

Working on
the Emotional Body

You begin by examining all your secrets, your secret fears and apprehensions. Then you release your "ugly side," your shadow side. Release all the things you hate about yourself. Release all the things that are not you, but that you do anyway. Ask yourself if you really want to forgive. Then ask why you want to forgive? If you want to forgive, then you begin to examine your actions. It's your actions, or the feelings behind them that you have to forgive. And you have to be brutally honest with your reality. You must examine yourself and see the things that are creating imbalances in your life, because anything that is creating imbalances in your life is preventing you from loving yourself. Write all these things down.

You must forgive, because non-forgiveness creates spiritual inertia and slows down your growth or transformation. Non-forgiveness gets suspended in time. What's in the past is still there, and what's in the future is already here, because the present contains the seeds of the past and the future. There is no past and there is no future. The present holds the key to your reality. So begin from your childhood to now and write all these things down.

Our emotions determine how we perceive other people, and how we perceive ourselves. Emotions are an outgoing-energy that carries a projection of the things we feel about other people. When you have intuitive insights into what your own individuality is about, you can respect and love yourself. Then you will be able to respect all those around you. Your individuality is your reality. Their individuality is their reality.

Working on the Mental Body

The second part of the process of self-forgiveness involves releasing your projections, your alignments, your identity. Begin to release your individuality, so your emotions can be exposed. If you cannot do this, the price of identifying with other people outside yourself is that you must live up to the image other people have of you. You have to release all the projections you place onto other people. Also, release the things that prevent forgiveness, like worry, guilt, and depression. They are only different forms of anger:

- Worry is anticipation. It makes you angry because you have this anticipation.

- Guilt derives from the anger you feel about yourself for having the feelings you brought on yourself.

- Depression occurs when you are in an abusive situation that is beyond your control. This, in turn, brings on anger. The anger behind worry, guilt, and depression comes, in essence, from your trying to seek retribution.

Every image, every projection, every boundary grows and stretches, but you set the tone, you set the image, you set the boundary. Images precede reality. Conception precedes manifestation. The absolute precedes phenomena. What is your image of yourself? How do you see yourself, your gender, your ancestry, and so forth? These are your alignments. They create your individuality and cause your emotions to be so tightly knitted together that it becomes difficult for you to expose your emotions. When you expose your images of yourself, your alignments and your projections, you free yourself from identifying with others, from identifying with images outside of yourself. Become free and take the responsibility for your own reality. You are not a victim but a co-creator.

Working on the Physical Body

The three components of self-forgiveness are observation, reaction, and action. How do you react to people and the world around you?

Self-forgiveness entails making the choice to change how you react to the actions of others. This creates new images. Now you are releasing all the things you have developed as a human being and you are now becoming a spiritual being.

Self-forgiveness is a process of realigning yourself, of realigning your reality, of going down the middle of the road and trying to maintain harmony in your life. It is a process of going from left to right, from the material to the spiritual, trying to move with balance, trying to move with the flow. For the two are but two halves of the one reality you are making for yourself.

Self-forgiveness is a state of feeling, much as spirituality is a state of being. Spirituality cannot be pre-defined; it is a reality that you create. Spirituality doesn't mean you can do what your teacher can do. It means you can live your own reality and not follow in the footsteps of someone else. You simply live your reality; you don't meditate upon it.

All of these steps are just stepping-stones to another dimension. There is no ultimate goal. Everyone has the Tao; you just have to ignite the spark of consciousness and being, and tap into the source. If you look for a guarantee, understand that your ego and subconscious mind will show you all the reasons why you shouldn't change. We are not victims; we are the ones responsible. Reality exists only in the eyes of the individual who is seeing it.

Working with the Spiritual Body

The fourth step in the process of self-forgiveness is the beginning of the process of self-love. As you can now perceive that you are open to the energy of the Tao, you will also perceive and acknowledge the Tao all around you.

12

Love and Self-Love

You can spend many hours in workshops or reading books on spirituality. Ultimately, they say the same thing: the answer is love. Even though love is the answer, it is often the problem, as well, because many of us have a preconception of what love is. This has led many of us to restrict what love really is. Here, we'll talk about the many levels of love, the qualities of love, and of loving ourselves. I won't give you definitions. Rather, I'll make clearer the multiple dimensions of love.

We must first rid ourselves of all preconceptions about what love is and our feelings of what love ought to be, and try to experience what love really is. Love has many facets. Like spiritual understanding, it involves many levels of consciousness and being. As shown by the Pa Qua (figure 3, p. 140),

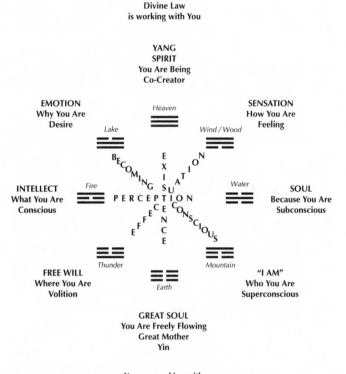

Figure 3. You Are—Pa Qua. You must balance both sides of each axis to bring yourself into harmony. How? Own it. The Taoist stands in the middle of the eight subtle energies of the Pa Qua, and, through prayer, meditation, and self-work, brings the eight subtle energies into balance. Polar Axes are from *The I Ching and the Genetic Code*, by Martin Schönberger (Santa Fe, NM: Aurora Press, 1979), pp. 52–55.

you can love every aspect of yourself: love of self as soul, love of self as "I Am," or spirit, love of internalized master or deity as higher self, etc. We'll see what love is, in some of its aspects, in relationship to others.

It is true that it is due to a lack of love that we don't grow spiritually. There is always room to love ourselves more. Therefore, we will form a perspective here on what love is, just as we now have a perspective on what spirituality is.

Just as spirituality is simply a relationship you have with yourself, love, too, is a relationship you have with yourself, a relationship that your consciousness has with your being. This is not narcissism, but rather self-love—the ability to truly open up to love within your being so that you can get to the root of yourself, so you can ask yourself, "What does it mean to love myself?" This must occur before you can even try to love anything or anyone beyond yourself.

First of all, what is love? One of the most important issues of our society today is how love is expressed through the mass media. Many of us learn about love in its more negative aspects, by observing love as it is expressed through guilt, pain, and suffering. What many of us know as love is being used, taken advantage of, taken for granted, and denying our own existence. When we deny our own existence, we become servants to love. We try to do anything we can possibly do to get it. Why? Because if we deny our own existence for love, we try as much as possible to derive our existence from love somewhere else. We will try to look for love, we'll try to find it, and, if it is not acknowledged by others, we say, "What do you mean, I don't love you? Look how much I've sacrificed for you, look how much I've given up for you." Many of us feel that sacrifice is a quality of love, that is suffering, pain, and agony are all qualities of love. So we say, "Considering how bad I feel, how can you say I don't love you?" When you listen to love songs on records and look at daytime soap operas, you see that love is agony, love is pain, love is suffering. Love is not something wonderful. It always involves hurt. You have to throw all these preconceptions of love right out the window. How else can you be open to the experience of what love is?

Some of us may feel there is an emptiness inside ourselves, and we look outside for something to fill that emptiness, to get the love we lack within ourselves. By doing that, we, program what love is, and also what love is not. We burn ourselves out looking for love. Those of us who seek love like this tend to ask the question, "Why can't I find someone to love me? Why can't I find love?" It is because you have clearly defined the parameters of your program of what love is, and how you will accept love. You then look for that particular program, and, when you can't find it, you feel you are not being loved. You feel you haven't found love.

Some of us, of course, will only surrender to loving ourselves in defeat. "If no one loves me, then I will love myself. But first, let me try to find someone who will love me." Why do we do this? All of us want to belong; we want to overcome separation. All of us want some way to communicate and interact with the world, to show the world our relevance. By seeking love, we seek relevance. We seek to know that someone else cares about us, and that we have an impact on that person. This gives us a sense of relevance, that what we do is meaningful to someone else. By seeking our relevance outside, however, we lose touch with how relevant we are to ourselves, what impact we have on ourselves.

We may say, "How I relate to my reality is not the important issue in my life. I want someone else who cares about me and my reality. I want someone else to talk to, to communicate with, to interact with. I want someone else to be intimate with." How can we achieve this if we are not intimately involved with ourselves first? That is the crucial thing.

When we define love outside of ourselves, we define our relevance to the world before us. It's definitely easier to love someone else than it is to love yourself. Society tells us to do that all the time. Society tells us to look at the homeless, look at the starving, look at the people who are sick. These are the people that we should give love to.

It is very easy to say, "Go out into the world and love someone else." There are so many causes. Each one of us has a cause in which we truly believe outside of ourselves, one that allows us to express our love.

Your first cause, however, should be yourself, because the causes you see outside yourself are reflections of the causes you see within yourself. To love yourself is to develop that relevance to who you are and what you believe in, regardless of what is happening outside. You will be relevant because of your own significance, your own impact that you have in your life. Those of us who choose the path of service may go out to save the world. We only begin to question this commitment when we begin to seek our relevance and begin to seek more and more out of our service. Love, however, is not something we give so that we can receive. Love is not associated with an action; love is a state of being. Love is a process within yourself, just like spirituality. You have to ask yourself, "What love is happening inside of me? Do I truly love myself? When can I truly love someone else?" You have to ask yourself that. Maybe some of us need others to love us first, before we can love ourselves. Loving ourselves is perhaps one of the greatest contributions that we can make to the world.

The greatest contribution you can make is to take responsibility for yourself, and to love yourself. That is the greatest contribution you can ever make to the world, because, by doing that, you know who you are, you know your significance, you know your impact. You know your relevance to the world, because you begin to love yourself. Then you belong in the world. You have significance. If you do love yourself, however, you have to do it in a way that counts, in a way that's total, in a way that brings results. You have to make an effort, at least in the beginning, to understand what that love is, and know how you will express it. You have to feel it in your heart, in your mind, in your totality. Remember, it is not about doing; it's a state of being.

The Chinese say you "be" so that you can know, so that you can do. Many of us study something so that we can know about it, so that we can become it. In Chinese philosophy it's always the opposite. You always "be" it first. If you can be it, and you know it, then you can do it. If you try to learn it, so that you can know it and then you can be it, you are already placing the goal beyond yourself. You have to acknowledge what you are at this particular moment. Spirituality is in the present; love is in the present. It's not something you learn to do. Many of us think that we can learn to love. Love is an expression. It's a conveyance of what you feel; it's a positive expression of your beingness. There are many things that can stop you from loving. Many times, we feel we do not deserve love. We may feel a lack of self-worth. That feeling then defines our reality. You have to first feel that you deserve what love is. Some of us feel we haven't earned it. We often feel we have to earn love. We feel we have to gain self-worth, so that we feel worthy of it. There is a lack of self-respect. So we begin to pity ourselves. Then we are not able to love. All of these things lead us to deny the livingness, because to be able to feel self-worth, self-respect, and self-esteem, we have to acknowledge the livingness that's inside of our being, the beauty that's inside of us, the love of self, the life force, the Tao.

Qualities of Love and Self-Love

The first thing we have to do is to get the definitions of what love is out of our program. No one is really an authority on love. Only you know what love is all about for you. Love is not based on what you do: it's not a state of doing. Love is based on how you feel, a state of being of which you are a vital part. Love, therefore, has many qualities, and these are the same qualities as spirituality. Love, in essence, defines what spiritual understanding is. Now we are going to talk about the qualities of love, and what it means to love ourselves. Some of the qualities of love are responsibility and respect, regard, truthfulness, trust, humility, patience, and commitment.

Responsibility, Respect

To begin with, you have to take responsibility for yourself, you have to be responsible for your life. One thing that goes hand-in-hand with responsibility is respect, because the more you become responsible for yourself, the more you begin to appreciate and respect yourself. That's why respect and responsibility always go hand-in-hand: "As I become more responsible, I begin to appreciate myself for taking the initiative in accepting my life's duty. This opens me to my life's work to fulfill my destiny, so that I gain respect for myself." Not only do you begin to respect yourself, you also begin to respect those around you. You begin to respect evolution, and you begin to respect that there are many levels of consciousness and being. Whatever someone does, you respect them for doing it, and you don't infringe upon them. One of the problems for those who take responsibility for themselves is that they expect everyone else around them to take responsibility for themselves as well. If those around them don't, they criticize, playing God, and judging. They try to decide what evolution should be for those other persons. Taking responsibility for yourself is strictly for yourself. You don't try to make someone else take responsibility for what he or she is. You respect the person because that goes hand-in-hand with who the person is. Not only do you begin to respect yourself, but, as you become aware that there are many levels of consciousness and being, you begin to respect those around you. You begin to respect evolution. Not only do you respect yourself for the initiative that you have taken, but you also respect others for what they are going through. Even if they are following someone else's path, even if they are following someone else's definitions, you respect them for it. You don't try to change them, for, by changing them, you are judging their evolution, you are infringing, and one of the keys of spirituality is non-infringement. You never infringe on someone else.

Respect is realizing that there is no "wrong way." In saying this, we are not giving license to infringement of any kind, but, as this is the realm of free will, we are all held accountable by divine law. The law of non-infringement levels the playing field for everybody. This is the way of evolution. If some people do something wrong, they have a chance to learn from their mistakes. You should not be judgmental of that. This allows them the opportunity to change, to be more.

Regard

Regard is a very special word when used in a spiritual context. Regard is having the humility to acknowledge the divine in all creation. In Hinduism, the sacred books use the

Sanskrit word *sraddha* to express this. The closest translation for it in English is "regard." An explanation of sraddha is given in the introduction to *Bhakti Rasamrita Sindu*, or Nectar of Devotion, that says one can live a devotional life of 100 years of sincere prayer and worship, and still not get to first base in spiritual life without it. You get regard from those who have it. It is this regard that opens the heart to the internal worship of the Lord. In this context, regard means regard for your self, for your teacher and for holy men, for fellow travelers, for your fellow men and women, for all sentient beings, and for the Way.

Ultimately, you learn that the world is a school, and this reality that you are in is part of the curriculum you have to take. Everything in your reality is part of your curriculum, and you have to grow with it. Some of us might get left back, because we don't want to accept the curriculum; we don't want to accept that reality. Many of us may transcend and go beyond that. The fact is, however, that, as you begin to respect yourself, you begin to honor and you begin to appreciate who you are and what you feel about your self.

Truthfulness

When you are responsible, you are being truthful to yourself. It is an act of truth to the reality of now. It bestows on you a sense of dignity, in which you perceive your reality without infringing upon someone else's. You are trying to develop your potentialities, and your potentialities are limitless. We can do anything we want to do in this world, as this is the realm of free will. So anything can be a part of our reality. When we take responsibility for ourselves, we do not need to challenge or debate someone else. Often, we feel that we take the responsibility for ourselves and someone else doesn't. Or someone else does something that we feel is not responsible. We feel their actions are questionable, and we see them get away with them. When we question someone else's reality, what are we doing? Either we are questioning our own reality or theirs. But it's still our reality. What is true for me may not be true for someone else. In essence, there is no absolute truth, because our truth is constantly changing. If we challenge what is truth now, we challenge the reality that is at this present moment. The reality we challenge is our perception, our reality. A fact is anything that is unable to change, and since our reality is constantly changing, it is not a fact. Reality can only be fact at a given moment; in the next moment, it can be an illusion. Something that is a fact right now may be totally wrong in the next moment. Responsibility and love make us honest about what we are to ourselves. We become very truthful to ourselves. And by becoming truthful, we become very secure.

Trust

We begin to trust ourselves because we feel responsible for who we are. But ask yourself, can you trust yourself 100 percent, right now? If you can trust yourself 100 percent right now, what happens to all of your problems? What happens to all of your insecurities? They disappear. If you trust yourself 100 percent, there are no problems. Everything will be as it should. But none of us trust ourselves 100 percent. There is always a shadow of a doubt somewhere. So, what we must do is try to become responsible for ourselves. This gives us trust and helps us to promote the practice of love. Likewise, when you tell your loved ones something that you feel is for their own good, although it may hurt them, you are telling them out of a feeling of responsibility to them and to yourself. It is the responsibility that gains the love. If what you tell them makes them feel afraid, or feel shame, or feel a lack of trust, or make them feel insecure or abandoned, that's not love. But if you do it out of responsibility to yourself and to them, then it gains the love that permeates between people.

Humility

The quality of humility is an extension of respect. To be humble is to see a person as the moment is. To be humble is to see the situation as the moment is. To be humble is to allow the opportunity for the moment to be more. That's what humility is all about—a willingness not to assume that just because something was, it will be. That's being humble. Being humble is taking the moment and allowing it to be more—not necessarily better, but always more. You give the person an opportunity to change. That's what humility and humbleness is about. If you want to be intimate, you have to be humble.

Why don't miracles happen? Miracles cannot happen if you already expect them not to happen. If you do not have a shadow of a doubt, you allow reality the opportunity to be more. It is through humility that miracles really happen. To be intimate, to be open, to be love, is a miracle. You must be very humble to be more open, more intimate. Humility allows you to look at a person not for what that person was, but for what that person is and for what that person can be. You allow the person the opportunity to blossom and be more and more of him- or herself. If you do that, what happens? The love grows and you see the person as being more. And if you see people as being more, what happens to you? You become more with them. That is a growth pattern, and it is through humility that it happens. If you look at yourself, all of your aspects, you can see the treasures that can make you different at this moment. That's when miracles can happen. They happen when you say, "There is this part of me I never discovered, and I never allowed myself to express, and now that I express it, I am learning more about myself." That's being intimate. That's being open. That's being humble. That's allowing yourself to love yourself more. Even if you never before succeeded in giving yourself a chance, it may be now. Maybe now there's a chance, not hoping there's a chance, but knowing there's a chance. Not only does humility give you an opportunity, in the sense that you hope the opportunity will come (that this person will be more), humility is also a knowing that it is now. Even the "maybe" starts to fade: "It is now. Now is when I can be more; now is when I can be better. Now."

Patience

Although patience isn't hoping, to have patience is to have hope for many people. If that is the case, what happens to patience? Patience becomes a limitation. Patience becomes something that restricts you. Patience becomes time-consuming.

No matter how miserable or how happy you are, patience means that you can change. Humility means that you can be more, and patience means that you can change—that the way to be more is to be willing to change.

Patience is dealing with the moment and then moving on; you are no longer hoping. You realize you're not in the moment until you move on. Patience is the willingness to move on and not become stagnated within one point of existence. Patience isn't someday; patience is now. Perseverance is someday. Now is what patience is all about, now and moving on. But, of course, to move on requires that you become committed to yourself.

Commitment

Commitment, in everyday parlance, has become a scary word. Many of you are probably already committed to something or someone, in one way or another—perhaps to a person, perhaps to a cause, or perhaps even to an ideal. But what about to yourself? What about commitment to your own growth, to your own spiritual understanding, to your own love? Is everything that you're doing conveying more of your livingness, more of your love? That love is you. You feel it because you know it. You then begin to understand what commitment is all about. When you're committed, you know things will work out. Commitment is a knowing. You feel the livingness between you and your self, or maybe between you and someone else. You know that commitment resonates. This requires courage, not because you are taking a step into the unknown, but because you know. Commitment is feeling and knowing that you are on the right path, so to speak, that you are on the road. That's why you are committed in the first place, because you give it priority. If you don't think you are on the right path, you're not going to be committed to it. You have to have a sense of knowing, a sense of belief in what you are getting yourself involved in, or else you won't get involved. So commitment does require some type of knowing. It takes courage to really know, since you feel it deeply in your totality. Love has to count in every way—in your heart, in your mind, and in everything you do.

Commitment, in essence, is faith and trust. Knowing is faith and knowing is trust, and you know that these are the words that love entails. Faith, trust, responsibility, humility, patience—all of these things are qualities of love. When I say that commitment requires faith and trust, I mean that you trust all that you are; you support all that you are; you begin to allow all that you are to manifest in all that is. Your choices and your actions are one thing. I do not make a choice and then do an action. My choice and my action are one thing, and everything that I do is a reflection of that one thing—myself. The trust and the faith that I have are within me. When you have trust and faith in your self, you really begin to accept your evolution. You really begin to respect everything that is around you, because you realize that the world simply is the way it is. In your humility, however, you know that the world can always be more, that the world doesn't have to be a sad world. There are choices. That's why we teach, in spirituality, that there are choices. We can choose love over agony, or joy over pain. No one is better than anyone else is, because we do not judge. You do not judge when you begin to love yourself, because you love your whole being. You know that the most you can give to the world is simply love. That love is the love you experience within yourself. When you understand this, you can understand that every experience you have is a way to awaken you to something else. If you love your self, everything that happens around you is permeated with that love. This makes your love stronger; it makes your love for your self greater. That greater love opens another level of consciousness and being; it allows you to go to another level of awakening, a greater realization through love.

Spirituality is, therefore, always in relationship to the reality you see before you. You can choose how you will walk, how you will relate. When you come into positive relationship with the Divine as higher self, the quality of your love for the Divine becomes more personal and begins to take on the quality of the Divine's love for you . . . Agape, Tao.

Celibacy and Sexuality

In the early stages of spiritual life, you learn the value of celibacy in overcoming your attachment to sex. Later in life, you find this detachment invaluable when you need to engage in a task for which celibacy is an essential requirement. Artists, athletes, initiates and others often sublimate their sexual energy and use its creative impetus to make manifest their creations in the world. Exercises like Tai Chi Chuan or Chi Kung can keep your energy moving and in balance. Celibacy is also of value when you are between relationships. Sexual promiscuity between relationships, even to practice the transformation of sexual energy is not desirable, because it leaves binding karmic attachments that you may have to live through at some time in the future. When a couple is in a positive loving relationship, the partners can seek material on the principles of Taoist cultivation of sexual energy to add a new and higher dimension of sexuality to their relationship.

The Taoist teaching on sexuality is that everyone is born with a certain amount of source ching or creative energy that is meant to last an entire lifetime. If you exhaust your source ching or sexual energy, you will lose vitality. This can lead to a breakdown in your health, to sickness, and to premature death.

Ching, or sexual energy, is the creative energy given to us by the Creator. Taoists teach that sex is a sacred act, and its offspring are sacred gifts from the Creator. Most orthodox religion teaches that sex should only be used for procreation—all other sexual encounters are considered acts of promiscuity. In India, the paths of Tantra, a branch of Shiva and Shakti worship, and the esoteric branch of Radha Krishna worship called *Sahaja*, both consider the sexual act sacred and dedicate it to the divine.

Taoists also teach that the sexual act is sacred and should only be used for procreation and transformation. A couple can dedicate the act to conceive a child in the world, or to bring about a transformation within one's own being. The book, *The Inner Teachings of Taoism*, tells us:

> In the path of cultivating reality, the thousand classics and ten thousand texts just teach people to harmonize

yin and yang, to cause yin and yang to merge and return to one energy. Observe how in the world husband and wife meet; when they mate, then they can
produce a child. In cultivation of the Tao, yin and yang
meet, and then when they mate, they can produce an
immortal.[12]

This describes how to bring about the transformation of energy within one's being that makes one an
immortal.

It is taught that in order to have an auspicious child-
birth and a gifted child, you should give careful consider-
ation to the time of conception and the quality of energy
invited in. In *Bodhisattva of Compassion*, a book about the
mystical tradition of Kuan Yin and Her other manifestations, Blofeld speaks of a story he heard of a young couple
who found themselves destitute. They prayed to the Goddess Tara to save them. They promised that if She helped
them survive the harsh winter, they would bring the child
the wife was carrying (if it was a boy) to the local monastery. They were saved and the father brought his son to
the local monastery and offered him to the Goddess Tara
as promised. The novice-master, hearing that they had no
other children, said, "Since this is your only son and he

[12] Thomas Cleary, trans., *The Inner Teachings of Taoism*, with com-
mentary by Liu I-Ming (Boston: Shambhala, 1986), p. 31.

will be coming to us two years from now, you had best go back and make other sons, for your wife's sake if not your own. Tell your wife, by the way, that if she fervently whispers Tara's name when you are making children together, you are sure to have a lovely high-spirited daughter. Be sure to call her Tara, or Dolma, if you prefer."[13] These teachings of Tara, or Kuan Yin in another form, are part of the Buddhist and Taoist traditions.

---

[13] John Blofeld, *Bodhisattva of Compassion* (London: Allen & Unwin Ltd., 1977–1978), p. 59.

Taoist Mysticism

Spirituality is our relationship with the reality that is before us at this moment. That relationship can be one of acceptance or denial. I can simply deny certain aspects of my reality and say this is not part of my life, this is not how I should be at this moment. When we do this, we are denying the livingness within ourselves, the ability to grow beyond what we are. We don't want to be what we are, so we are stopping the flow at this particular moment. To be able to accept who we are and the situations life puts us in requires the healing power of love. We must, therefore, learn how to love ourselves—that is the answer.

Unless we have the good fortune to meet a master who has developed and radiates this love, there is no one who can portray or teach us what love is. They can only describe certain qualities that are associated with love. The qualities that reinforce love are qualities that allow us to be very modest, to have a sense of trust, to have a sense of security, to have faith, patience, humility, and regard—all qualities associated with love.

Spirituality, however, is also about evolution. It is about how we are evolving, what we are being, what we are becoming. It is how we look at evolution and how we are trying, to the best of our understanding, to be a part of that evolution. Many of us cannot be a part of evolution, so we tend to fight it. We cannot accept the reality that is before us and we cannot accept the reality that is outside of us. So many of us seek images outside ourselves to fulfill this evolutionary pattern.

It's Love, working with evolution, that creates the transformation that takes place through spiritual understanding. Through this transformation, we begin to understand livingness, for by understanding love and evolution, we understand life. We understand that life is always abundant. Life is not a denial; it is not something that denies the livingness.

If we associate love with guilt and suffering, we may say to ourselves, "I've spent all my life doing these things for this person, and this person doesn't recognize me, this person doesn't appreciate me, this person doesn't honor me. I have given of myself and now I feel myself lessened."

We must understand that love does not make us feel less, it makes us feel more. It takes away all of the pain.

You may have been taught that in spiritual understanding, you have to go through pain and suffering to find love. In truth, you do not have to discover love through agony, pain, and suffering. Love is not a choice that you make; it is a part of the being that you are. If your life is suffering, then it's because part of your reality has created this.

In essence, we are talking about transforming life; this is what we are trying to do. In transforming our lives, as we grow, as we mold and realign ourselves, we find that the basis of this realignment is survival. We do this because we want to survive. If you examine your life at any moment, if you access the things that are happening in your life at that moment, you may say there are a lot of things you would never do again. Ultimately, when you examine and access your life, it becomes a cluster of memories of moments that make it seem meaningful, and moments that make it seem tragic. In essence, what you are looking at are moments when you felt the need to survive, the need to find meaning for survival, the need to find some purpose, some type of relevance, some type of significance to make your stand in the world. For all of us want to make an impact. We want to make ourselves feel fully human, to make ourselves feel fully alive.

How do we feel fully human? What we are examining is what we can do with ourselves, because the greatest loss is not the loss of human life, but the loss of human potential, what we can do with our lives. If you lose the opportunity to live up to your fullest potential, that is the greatest tragedy of all.

The greatest challenge in life is to form a relationship with your higher self that is deep, meaningful, and lasting. Then you can honor yourself, then you can appreciate yourself, then you can love yourself as you evolve, as you survive life. If you use the evolutionary pattern, it enables you to create this relationship, and expand it to create relationships with those around you that are meaningful and longlasting. This becomes the greatest challenge in life.

Ultimately, it always comes back to love and what love is. It is the lack of love that prevents you from being spiritual. It is the refusal to let go of the past, the refusal to forgive, that binds you. You may say, "I do not want to let go of the past, because there is too much hurt in the past," but by not letting go of the past, you have stopped the flow. You can't move on because you are being pulled back, so it's a tug of war. You need to establish a balance in your life to be able to live in the now.

It is also your ego that denies you the greater you, because the ego provides security in your life. To have faith, you shatter the ego and the need for security. To have faith

100 percent, you can go into unknown areas, but going there with a sense of knowing this is what you have to do. The ego can not interfere with that.

Spirituality is, in essence, the concept the Taoists call Wu Chi—the concept of emptiness. Wu Chi is represented as something that is about to manifest, but hasn't yet manifested. Spirituality manifests through us, by the way that we make use of our lives, and our beings. Through our love and evolution, the way that we are being, we become. This represents Tai Chi, or the way of being whole, because love and respecting evolution makes us whole.

As we transform life through survival by trying to create meaning, we have created yin and yang. We have created the relativity of this world. We have created the things that make this world meaningful to us. In a way, each of us is like a spider that spins a web and lives in it until it dies, until its reality is shattered, until the web is gone. The things we pull to us, the things that we have around us, make up the web that we spin. Like a spider, we are spinning this web, creating a reality. Whatever comes to that web, comes to it because the web is there. That's your reality, so it pulls the things to you. If that is the case, you are in control of your reality. Then you can take the responsibility for your life. That means there are literally no impossibilities in this world. Remember, thought creates reaction; it creates actions that eventually follow the thought. You have to conceive of something first before it can manifest. Therefore, Tao literally comes from Wu Chi, emptiness. It comes from nothing. If we have an intent, it is manifested. The thought precedes the action and the reaction to it. It also precedes the manifestation. If you control your thoughts, you can control your actions and, eventually, reactions, to manifest a new reality.

PART 3

Sam Ching
(Three Realms of Being)

Knowing The Eternal Law
(The Universal Law Of Nature—The Inner Law Of Man)

Attain the utmost in Passivity,
Hold firm to the basis of Quietude.
The myriad things take shape and rise to activity,
    But I watch them fall back to their repose.
Like vegetation that luxuriantly grows
    But returns to the root (soil) from which it springs.
To return to the root is Repose;
    It is called going back to one's destiny.
Going back to one's Destiny is to find the Eternal Law.
To know the Eternal Law is Enlightenment.
And not to know the Eternal Law
    Is to court disaster.
He who knows the Eternal Law is tolerant;
Being tolerant, he is impartial;
Being impartial, he is kingly;
Being kingly, he is in accord with Nature;

Being in accord with Nature, he is in accord with Tao;
Being in accord with Tao, he is eternal,
And his whole life is preserved from harm.

—*The Wisdom of Laotse*[14]

---

[14] Lin Yutang, *The Wisdom of Laotse* (New York: Modern Library, 1976), p. 109.

15

Taoist Cosmology
As Above So Below
As Below So Above
A Hermetic Truth

The whole manifestation of creation, from the One to the ten thousand things is seen through the eight trigrams of the *I Ching*, which, when multiplied together, form the hexagrams creating the sixty-four changes. Starting from Wu Chi, the source, yang energy from the Creator divides itself in two, establishing yang and yin, or the masculine and feminine principles. Then the two energies divide into four energies, into greater (or moving) yang, smaller (or resting) yin, smaller (or resting) yang; and greater (or moving) yin. This establishes the four elements of the subtle realm in the Chinese system (see figure 4, page 170).[15]

---

[15] Figures 4, 5, and 6 are redrawn from *Moving with Change*, by Rowena Patte (New York: Arkana, 1986), pp. 242–243.

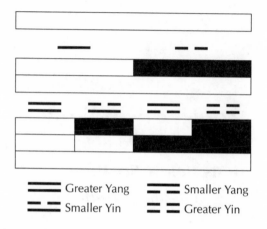

Greater Yang | Smaller Yang
Smaller Yin | Greater Yin

Figure 4. The four elements of the subtle realm.

The four elements are metal or air, fire, water, and wood or nature (see figure 12, page 216). The energies of the four elements divide into the eight subtle energies of Tai Chi and the eight trigrams of the *I Ching*. The eight trigrams are symbols that represent all that happens in Heaven and on Earth (see figure 5, page 171).

Pa Qua—
The Before Heaven Sequence

Five thousand years ago, when Fu Hsi was formulating the *I Ching* from insights he received from the patterns on a tortoise shell, he took the eight trigrams and placed the first four

Figure 5. The eight trigrams of the *I Ching*.

counter-clockwise around the left side of a circle. Going up the center of the circle, he brought the last four trigrams around the right side of the circle in a clockwise fashion, in such a way that the yin lines compliment or balance the yang lines of the trigrams across from them (see figure 6, page 172). If you look at the three lines of each trigram on one side of the circle, where there is a solid line in the trigram on one side of the circle, there is a broken line in the trigram on the other side, and vice versa. The eight balanced energies here represent the energies in the Mind of the Creator, or The Before Heaven Sequence. Since the energies of all the trigrams are balanced in the mind of the Creator, if we can bring our own minds to this balanced state, we come into union with the energy of the Creator and become open to the source.

The eight trigrams represent the first three steps into the realm of Tai Chi from the source. Now we take three more steps into the realm of yin/yang, and the sixty-four hexagrams, or changes, of the *I Ching*.

Figure 6. The eight balanced energies of the *I Ching*.

From the eight energies of Tai Chi, we go to sixteen energies, representing the yin and the yang of each of the eight subtle energies. From these sixteen energies, we go to thirty-two energies, with Earth making the thirty-third energy of the Taoist system. From these thirty-two, we go to the sixty-four changes of yin/yang (see figure 7, page 173).

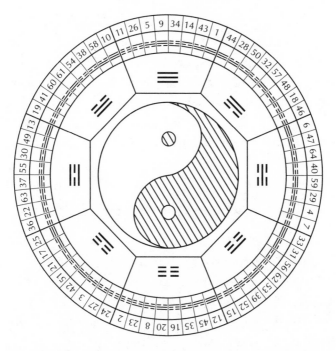

Figure 7. The eight energies and the sixty-four changes of yin/yang. Redrawn from *The Book of Changes and the Unchanging Truth*, by Hua Ching Ni (Santa Monica, CA: Shrine of the Eternal Breath of Tao, 1983), p. 15.

Yin/Yang

When the original energy of light came from the source, it refracted on the subtle atmosphere of Tai Chi into eight rays or energies. When these eight rays or energies enter the atmosphere of yin/yang, this material world, they refract on themselves to form the sixty-four hexagrams or changes. This is interesting, because it begins to give us an insight into how the Creator's energies manifested in this world. We hear people say, "Well, God made everything, so God is in everything." But how do we know it? In our meditations, we can feel this, but to know it is another matter.

The *I Ching* and the Genetic Code

Some years ago, Dr. Martin Schönberger wrote a book called *The I Ching and the Genetic Code*, which illustrates the parallels between the structure of the *I Ching* and that of the Genetic Code. The following excerpt from Schönberger's book outlines the astonishing similarities between the natural science of the *I Ching* and the latest discoveries of nuclear genetics.

Natural Science "FORM" The Genetic Code: "The Book of Life" John Kendrew	Philosophical Theory "CONFIGURATION" "The Book of Changes"
	Compendium of natural philosophy from ancient China, compiled by Fu Hsi and edited by Confucius

1. Discovered [48] years ago, has existed since life began. All the vital processes of all living creatures whose structure, form and heredity are programmed in precise detail *universal claim* [*sic*].

2. The basis is the plus and minus double helix of DNA

3. Four letters are available for labeling this double helix: A-T, C-G, (adenine, thymine, cytosine, guanine), which are joined in pairs

4. Three of these letters at a time form a code word for protein synthesis

5. The "direction" in which the code words are read is strictly determined ($\longrightarrow$)

6. There are 64 of these triplets known whose property and informative "power" has been explored. One or more triplets program the structure of one of the possible 22 amino ac-

1. All processes of living development throughout nature are subject to *one* strictly detailed program (*universal,* physical, metaphysical, psychological, moral *claim*)

2. The basis is the manifestation of the world principle in the primal poles yang (——) and yin (- -)

3. Four lines suffice for life in all its fullness.
   7=resting yang ———
   9=moving yang — o —
   8=resting yin   —   —
   6=moving yin   — x —

4. Three of these lines at a time form a trigram, a primary image of the 8 possible dynamic effects

5. The "direction" in which the trigram is read is strictly determined ($\uparrow$)

6. There are 64 double trigrams precisely designated and described by Fu Hsi (3000 B.C.) in very vivid and precise images of highly specific dynamic states (e.g. "break-

ids; quite specific sequences of such triplets program the form and structure of all living creatures, from the amoeba to the iridescent peacock's feather

through" or "oppression") within each case 6 possible variations of this state and subsequent transformation into another one of the 64 hexa—grams—a program of fate, as it were, in which each individual is at all times placed to operate the "switch" of fate from which point onwards the "train" continues along its appointed "line"

7. Two of these triplets have names: "beginning" and "end." They mark the beginning and end of a code sentence of some length.

7. Two hexagrams have names: before completion—after completion (frequently opening and closing "melodies of fate" in the oracle).[16]

Figure 8 shows a table (from *The Inner Structure of the I Ching,* by Lama Anagarika Govinda, published in Trumbull, CT, by Weatherhill in 1981) that illustrates how the 64 hexagrams of the *I Ching* correspond to the 64 triplets in the gentic code. Below the table is a list of amino acids and their abbreviations, which also appear in the table. The two codes are shown in binary order (according to Martin Schönberger).

So the question we have to ask is: what is involved here? Are both "books" manifestations of a common principle?

---

[16] Martin Schönberger, *The I Ching and the Genetic Code* (Santa Fe, NM: Aurora Press, 1979), pp. 31–35.

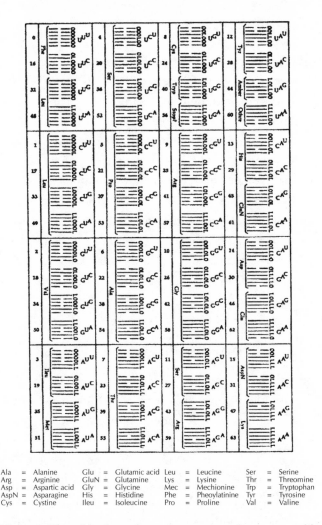

Ala	=	Alanine	Glu	=	Glutamic acid	Leu	=	Leucine	Ser	=	Serine
Arg	=	Arginine	GluN	=	Glutamine	Lys	=	Lysine	Thr	=	Threomine
Asp	=	Aspartic acid	Gly	=	Glycine	Mec	=	Mechionine	Trp	=	Tryptophan
AspN	=	Asparagine	His	=	Histidine	Phe	=	Pheoylatinine	Tyr	=	Tyrosine
Cys	=	Cystine	Ileu	=	Isoleucine	Pro	=	Proline	Val	=	Valine

Figure 8. The table above shows the genetic code represented by the hexagrams of the *I Ching*. The two codes are shown in binary order (according to Martin Schönberger). Below the table is a list of the amino acids and their abbreviations.

Is there perhaps one universal code which was discovered 5,000 years ago by the Chinese and 48 years ago by Watson and Crick? Is there only one spirit whose manifestation must of necessity find its expression in the 64 words of the genetic code, on one hand, or in the 64 possible states and developments of the *I Ching* on the other? Is there one law running through the whole of nature in all its diverse physical, spiritual, intellectual, and moral processes as determined by fate? This realization as glimpsed through the eyes of the physician gives us a scientific insight into a world, whole and sound, undivided by discord, where physics and metaphysics are one—resulting, in security, calm, and happiness.

From Tai Chi to Wu Chi

Through the light of the *I Ching*, we begin to gain the ability to see the hand of the Creator, and how the Creator manifested this world. To know how we got here is to know the way home. The eight trigrams symbolize the eight energies of the Pa Qua, which are constantly undergoing change as they are manifesting into the world from the source. On our journey home, therefore, we are going from the world back to the source through Tai Chi and the process of transformation, symbolized by the eight energies of Pa Qua—coming back into balance to rest in the One.

In The Before Heaven Sequence of the Pa Qua, the yin energy counterbalances the yang energy on each axis in the mind of the Creator. At the time of creation, the Great Mother transmutes her spiritual energy of Quest to her material energy and pulls the Yang energy of Spirit into manifestation, for the sake of all the spirit-souls seeking rebirth and transformation. When we become seekers, we come in tune with her energy of Quest. Through the energy of Quest, we transform our yin energy to yang. The energy of Quest transmutes material energy to attract the yang energy of spirit, or higher self; it is like our reaching in for spirit and spirit reaching out to us.

The Four Elements

Now we'll extend the four elements into the material realm and link them to the Western system and Jung's depth psychology, so we can work with his four psychological types. We have already spoken about the four elements in the Chinese system (see page 170). These four elements are in the subtle realm, where metal (or air) is opposite wood (or nature), and fire is opposite water. When they come into the gross realm, they go through a change. When we work with the four elements in the Western system, where the position of the elements is determined by their atomic weight, fire changes position with air, as fire is lighter than air. When we look at a diagram of the four elements in the Western system, fire is opposite the element earth, symbolized by wood (or nature), and air (or metal) is opposite water. In the Chinese system, the four elements therefore represent the four steps or the four disciplines of self on our four bodies. In the Western system, they represent the four psychological types. When you know your psychological type, then you also know its opposite type, of which you have least knowledge and control. You can begin to bring balance into your life by bringing light to your opposite psychological type that lies in the dark.

In the Taoist philosophical system, we work with the eight energies of the Pa Qua, which, multiplied by the four elements, make thirty-two energies. We take each of the four elements and put them in the center of a circle to form its own Pa Qua. If you are an air type, you can step into the center of a Pa Qua with air as its center and see how the energies of the Pa Qua feel around you. In the same way, you can work with each of the elements for each of the psychological types. Although we all have a dominant psychological type, we have the other three types within us as well. Eventually, we'll have to bring them all into balance.

Working with the four psychological types is similar to working with the Hindu "modes of nature." One must work to transcend the modes of ignorance, passion, and goodness to come into a self-realized state of consciousness.

The native peoples' vision quest is another example of investigating one's life experience while walking in the four directions—north, south, east, and west— representing the four aspects of self.

The same thing is true in living through each of the two nights: the dark night of the soul, and the dark night of the spirit. They are the internal initiations that the Great Mother puts us all through to awaken us to the reality of ourselves as spirit-souls. In this process, your ego, or conscious mind, will find itself in darkness. Out of necessity, you will have to rely on your soul-self and your instincts, to keep your emotions under control and keep you out of difficulty in the world. Through this process, you will gain the ability to rely on your intuition, to keep you in tune with the Great Mother and higher self, to get you through life's changes successfully. This internal process of integration and transformation will ultimately bring you to self-realization.

As the spiritual energy of Quest of the Great Mother brings in the New Age, those things that are now shrouded in darkness will begin to come into the light. That is the nature of the Great Mother's energy of Quest. With the dawn of the New Age, the transformational energy of Quest will progressively bring about a balancing of Earth's energy and all that are on it. This will seem, for each of us, like a group initiation, like a group dark night of the soul. There will be a chance for the faculty of intuition to become

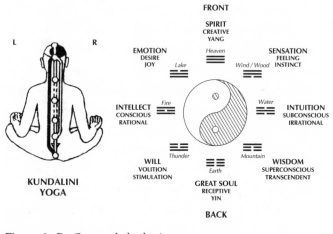

Figure 9. Pa Qua and the brain.

open to all, if we so choose, and everyone will have a chance for transformation.

The Pa Qua and the Brain

Figure 9, above, gives a diagram (on the left) from a system of Yoga that shows the *ida, pingala,* and *sushumna* nadis. The ida and pingala nadis represent the sympathetic nervous system, and the sushumna nadi represents the parasympathetic nervous system. The ida nadi, going up the left side of the figure, represents the Moon line, the past, and the feminine principle (see figure 9). The pingala nadi, going up the right side of the figure, represents the Sun line, the future, the masculine principle. The sushumna nadi, going up the middle or central nervous system, represents the middle way, the present. We see the ida crossing over at the upper tan tien to the back and right side of the brain, and the pingala crossing over at the upper tan tien to the front and left side of the brain. The sushumna functions much as the Taoist thrusting channel, in that it connects us with spirit. Metaphysically speaking, if we take a bird's eye view of the body, looking down at the top of the head, we find that the brain, as the physical representation of the mind, is a replica of the Pa Qua (see figure 9, right).

The Pa Qua and the Body

When we turn the diagram of the Pa Qua around 180 degrees, an interesting thing happens. We have the energies of the body represented as the twelve major meridians, plus the governor and conception vessels. The yang energy of the governor vessel goes up the back, and the yin energy of the conception vessel comes down the front. The yin meridians go to the internal organs of the body, and the yang meridians go to the external organs of the body. The energy of the two thrusting channels inside the

FRONT

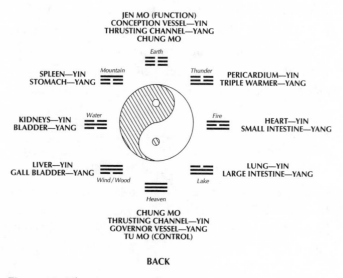

Figure 10. The sixteen meridians.

---

body completes the sixteen meridians. Most people don't have the thrusting channels open. When the thrusting channels are open, you have internal contact with deity. It is as though your head is open to Tai Chi, while your body is in yin/yang—like living in two realms at the same time (see figure 10).

16

Integration and Transformation

As is revealed in the Isis and Osiris myth, as well as in the Egyptian *Book of the Dead*, Set stands at the threshold of initiation. Isis and Osiris were lovers, but their half brother, Set, also loved Isis. Out of jealousy, he killed Osiris and dismembered his body. Isis magically, but briefly, restored life and potency to Osiris. She conceived a son named Horus. Years later, when Set was subdued and brought to justice by Horus, Isis refused to let Horus kill his uncle. So now Set stands at the temple door as the archetypal group shadow. All those who would come to the temple for initiation into spirit must pass by Set. Those with any of the qualities of Set, those who have not yet owned their own shadow, will be denied entrance by Set into the temple for initiation. As the temple can be an external place in the world, it can also be an internal place within your own heart. It is in the internal temple of the heart that this initiation will take place, enlightened by the highest intuitions of the mind or the "I Am," for heart represents the place where the soul's feeling nature has its highest expression. Likewise, mind, or the "I Am," represents the place where the soul's intuitive nature has its highest expression as spirit.

The Age Old Question, "Is the glass half empty or half full?"

In the past, as I was looking at my life, I saw how bad it was. My life situation wasn't entirely to my liking. I reflected on how to bring about positive change in my life, but I was looking on the outside, so I couldn't find a way. All I could see were the situations that were causing me much pain. In my reflection, I was told I was not seeing clearly; my angle of vision was faulty. I was told to look at my life from the position of higher self. Now I look at my life with new eyes, and all of a sudden, I realize how fortunate I am. I look at my life, and I can see all the potential, all the possibilities.

As we find ourselves here in this world, we try to find our place, where we belong. We labor under the assumption that this world is our home, but it's a school. We are like travelers passing through this world-school, gaining experience along the way. Although the Universal Law says you can be all you can be and to share in the world's abundance, you do it by taking your place in the Creator's plan, not in your own. When you become abundant, you begin to realize that everything you have is really given to you on loan, and you must give it back when you are ready to move on.

We have all made what might be called mistakes in the past, but we should look at them as lessons we had to learn in the school of life along the way. We try not to have to learn the same lessons over and over again. When the same lessons appear over and over again in different ways, like recurring themes in our lives, they take on a special significance. It is here that we have to sit still and meditate long to be able to discern the underlying root cause that has to be addressed. We have to be able to accept the bitter pill of strong medicine given to us by the Great Mother to correct that root cause. She is cracking the gross shell of our material existence and making our inside and outside one. As we venture beyond materiality, we step through Her veil of mist into the abyss and come into the place of unknowing. We find this place chaotic, as our reality starts to shift before us. We begin to release our fears by recognizing them as manifestations of our own internal shadows as we allow them to come out of the darkness of the night into the light of day. When we step beyond these fears, our subconscious minds try to pull us back with the question, "Will life really allow us to live and be free to be who we are, where we are, now?" These thoughts come, along with our prayers to the Great Mother to be free to be.

As we come into positive relationship with this Great Soul, we begin to come in tune with the realm of Tai Chi. As we begin to balance the yin and yang of each of the eight energies of the Pa Qua, we start to open up to Tai Chi. It is as though the world is opening to us and we are opening to the world. How scary, but how strangely wonderful it is! Here is where we connect with higher self and where we can become co-creators. We begin to realize we can control our reality, for we know that how we will spend tomorrow depends upon how we live today. Dare to live in the moment.

Integrating the Shadow or Yin Side of the Pa Qua

You find, as your body is your temple, the shadow stands just outside your threshold of consciousness, somewhere in the back of your head, waiting to grab you. So integrate it.

In 1917, in his essay "On the Psychology of the Un-conscious," Jung speaks of the personal shadow as the other in us, the unconscious personality of the same sex, the reprehensible inferior, the other that embarrasses or shames us:

"By shadow I mean the 'negative' side of the personality, the sum of all those unpleasant qualities we like to hide, together with the insufficiently developed functions and the content of the personal unconscious."[17]

Soul

Before we talk about the shadow, we must first talk about the soul. The soul is one of the most misunderstood parts or aspects of the self. On the Pa Qua, the soul is in the place of intuition, because soul gives us a sense of being. As we said before, soul is the energy that travels throughout your body and makes you you. It is a knowing kind of energy that, on deeper levels, links up with the Great Soul or the Great Mother of Earth and in the realm of Tai Chi. Through Her, it links up with the unconscious, and with group consciousness. Soul also links up through the "I Am," with higher self. The soul has special abilities: those of a psychic nature, dealing more with feelings, and those of an intuitive nature, dealing with a knowing. As most people live on the surface of life, they sel-

---

[17] Connie Zweig and Jeremiah Abrams, *Meeting the Shadow* (New York: J. P. Tarcher/Putnam & Sons, 1991), pp. 3–4.

dom dive deeply into themselves to experience soul, except in times of joy and sorrow.

In early life, we are all connected directly to our soul nature. We know who we are. As we grow older, however, most of us grow away from soul and those deeper levels of our being. This starts when we are children, for example, when we are afraid of the dark, experiencing those scary things that come up in our minds from the subconscious, especially on rainy nights during a thunderstorm, or after we watch a particularly scary movie. These experiences are generally laughed away by a brother, sister, or friend, who explains them away as coming from the boogieman. When these kind of experiences are not properly explained and resolved, they become something we try to keep from coming into our conscious mind by pushing them further down into the subconscious, thus creating a place for the shadow to form and develop. We add to this all those things about ourselves that are rejected as improper in our upbringing, and so begin creating our own phantoms and demons.

Shadow

Living through the experience of shadow work is the conscious part of the process of going through the dark night of the soul. As initiates delve into the realm of the Great Mother, they seem to be always in the dark, except for the

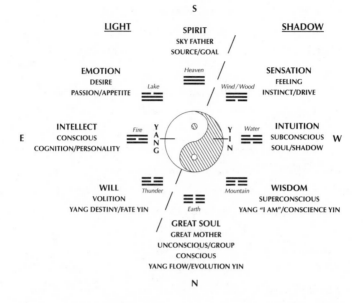

S

LIGHT — SHADOW

SPIRIT
SKY FATHER
SOURCE/GOAL

Heaven

EMOTION
DESIRE
PASSION/APPETITE

Lake

Wind / Wood

SENSATION
FEELING
INSTINCT/DRIVE

INTELLECT
CONSCIOUS
COGNITION/PERSONALITY

Fire

Y
A
N
G

Y
I
N

Water

INTUITION
SUBCONSCIOUS
SOUL/SHADOW

E

W

WILL
VOLITION
YANG DESTINY/FATE YIN

Thunder

Mountain

WISDOM
SUPERCONSCIOUS
YANG "I AM"/CONSCIENCE YIN

Earth

GREAT SOUL
GREAT MOTHER
UNCONSCIOUS/GROUP
CONSCIOUS
YANG FLOW/EVOLUTION YIN

N

Figure 11. Integrating the shadow side of Pa Qua. Ask yourself, "What is true mind for me?" Then start from there. Begin by placing your self in the center of the Pa Qua, and experience your feelings and emotions, your consciousness and your being, and own your self. Bring the yin and yang of all your parts of self into balance.

intuitive guidance of the Great Mother or higher self from the yin side of the realm of Tai Chi.

"In 1945," Zweig and Abrams tell us, "Jung was referring to the Shadow as simply the thing a person has no wish to be. 'One does not become enlightened by imagining figures of light,' he said 'but by making the darkness conscious. The latter procedure, however, is disagreeable and therefore not popular.'"[18]

Opening up to the shadow side is an individual affair. You can begin by looking at figure 11 (see page 191). This figure shows the two sides of the Pa Qua—the yang, or light side, and the yin, or Shadowy side. It also shows the yang and the yin of the eight aspects of the Pa Qua (yang/yin). Stand in the center of the Pa Qua and relate to its eight yang aspects as eight yang parts of yourself, as illustrated in figure 3 (see page 140). I have added the eight yin aspects of the Pa Qua, to which you can relate to as the eight yin parts of yourself.

The following is an example of bringing one's life into balance through integration of the self, by relating to the yang and the yin aspects of the self on the Pa Qua.

Allen, an older member of an interfaith community, was busy establishing loving relationships with other younger members and trying to be helpful in getting them properly situated in their spiritual life. However, the governing body of his community felt he was giving too much attention to one female member, and told him to end the association. With this, Allen told them,

---

[18] Zweig and Abrams, *Meeting the Shadow*, pp. 3–4.

"I am only trying to help her in her situation. If you would help her, there would be no need for me to go out of my way to help her." Then the pressure was applied to both of the members to end their association. Allen felt, since his motivation was pure and self-less, that he was being unfairly persecuted. Those looking on from outside, however, could clearly see some attachment on his part. Allen had a drinking problem and sought to release the pressure of the situation in that way. When he was called on the carpet for going on a drinking binge, he freely admitted it, but he felt there was no impropriety as far as the young woman was concerned. He felt that, if he was guilty of anything, it may have been that he was overprotective of the female member. So he went on a binge to escape the pain and frustration of the situation. Feeling hurt, disappointed, frustrated, and helpless, he felt that if he stayed in the community, a similar situation could unfold in the future. So, he left the interfaith community.

Now let's place Allen's life situation on the Pa Qua. If we look at his life—from the place of intelligent will, or volition (since this material world is the realm of free will), he can choose to continue to live a spiritual life. Or, out of self-pity, he can return to the life of an alcoholic and fall away from the spiritual platform that he is striving to establish in his life. Here is a clear choice between living from the higher self or from the lower self (yang or yin), taking the way of destiny or fate.

From the place of cognition, he felt a personal attack on his integrity and truthfulness, and he felt obliged to defend himself.

From the place of personality-self, with his good understanding of spiritual life, he could clearly see the governing body's stand against his position. His ego or personality-self got its feelings hurt. With his feelings hurt, he reacted as he had in the past—like a child on the instinctual level. He did what he felt necessary to escape the pain!

From the place of emotions, as his desire to serve the younger members was thwarted, he reacted by satisfying his senses instead of spirit.

From his soul-self, he knows the situation that he is in, and he is trying to deal with it rationally.

From his shadow-self, by his attack on the governing body, he found himself caught in a hopeless situation with no way out. He felt that there should have been some kind of recognition of his place as an older member of the community.

From his instinctual-self, since this was not forthcoming, he went on a binge and got intoxicated to relieve the pressure of a painful situation. He left the community.

From the place of conscience, he knows he was out of control getting intoxicated, but he felt the situation was hopeless.

From the place of his "I Am" or spirit, he felt he needed to make some kind of stand to uphold his position of integrity and truthfulness, and to reestablish his feeling of self-worth. He desires to do this from the place of his "I Am" or spirit, but he is not clear on how to do that.

In summary, since Allen does have firm faith in the Divine, in its dual aspects of God the Mother and the Father, they will provide the internal space to which he can go and find the solution he needs to sort this out. Then he will see clearly where the confusion lies.

That he reacted from his ego or personality-self, after being told by the governing body to end the association with the female member.

Then, from the place of shadow, he responded to them in an adverse way. By admonishing them for not helping the female member, he brought down their censure on himself.

From the place of emotions, with his desire to serve his fellow members thwarted, he served his lower self instead of his higher self.

Reacting from the place of instinctual-self, he got intoxicated.

Now he needs to bring these parts of self back into proper balance with the other parts of self, under the intuitive guidance of higher self or spirit. He needs to forgive the members of the governing body, his fellow members, and himself.

He has to gain the capacity to stand on his own two feet, with or without the association of the interfaith community. He needs to expand his spiritual practice to include the energy of compassion for all the members of the community. That is the quality of energy he needs to heal the hurt and the feeling of rejection.

The governing body of the interfaith community has subsequently asked Allen to return to the community, thus bringing a good conclusion to an unfortunate situation.

Working with the Pa Qua gives us a chance to bring each part of the self into the light of consciousness, so that we may deal with our life situations rationally.

First, you have to relate to the eight yang parts of yourself on the Pa Qua, then you have to relate to the eight yin parts of yourself on the Pa Qua. Tune in to those parts of yourself and see how they feel about going through this process of integration. In meditation, let each part speak, including conscience, the shadow, and instinctual-self. Each part of yourself speaks in its own way, through a feeling, an intuition, or a knowing, or perhaps through your sincere heart's desire. Let all parts of yourself know that you are undergoing a process of integration of the shadow side of your self. Then ask if any part has any objections. If there are objections, listen to them and patiently try to work them out. It may take some time for ego, shadow, or instinctual-self to accept, so keep trying. Once all parts of self agree to undergo this process of integration under the internal guidance of the Great Mother or higher self, the way is made clear to begin the process in earnest.

This process of integration can help push you into a deeper level within your being. The anxiety comes because this is where you repressed your shadow a long time ago. Like a long-caged animal, it wants to get out. This causes the anxiety, apprehension and fear. You have to keep firmly to your principles at these times to see you through the crisis. You must gain an understanding of who your shadow is and why it is there, so you can clear the way for integration. Shadow will then willingly surface into consciousness as the other half of soul. If you function from the place of child, the place of innocence, all will be revealed. In the place of the child, you have the capacity to dream, to wonder. The whole world of fantasy opens up for you, the place of gnomes and fairies, elementals and dragons— where angels and archangels are guardians. In the place of innocence, there is no mind, no need to have concern about grown-up worldly matters. You don't need to run after the shadow to integrate it, just be free to be part of the whole and the shadow will join in. What you see as shadow depends on where you are standing now.

Once you open up to your individual shadow, you find it's linked with your group shadow and with cultural shadows. In the process of owning your own shadow, you must find where your shadow connects with these group shadows. You have to bring them into consciousness as well and acknowledge their existence, without being judgmental, or they may manifest in the world around you. It is the Great Mother's way to bring the things that are in the darkness into the light, so you can see clearly what needs to be worked on to bring you into balance. So first, you need to relate to your group shadow and see what that is, and then to your cultural shadow and see how it relates to you.

Every culture has its shadow, and multi-cultures have multi-shadows, so you need to be clear about how, or if, they directly affect you and your "I Am" as spirit. Understand that a culture is a living entity with a capacity for growth and change. Here, however, we are talking about your growth, your transformation, your change. So the flip side is that you now begin to realize that the shadow side of a culture for you may represent a whole group of people walking another way. They have a right to their existence, too, just as you have a right to yours. As the old paradigm shifts, you begin to realize that those on the other side are not your adversaries. They just have a different world-view, a different reality. On that side, you may find some of your neighbors, friends, teachers, co-workers, even family. The paradigm shift of your consciousness from the place of ego or personality-self to you as a spirit-soul opens you up to be able to forgive and to have compassion. This is a testing time of your personal resolve and inner strength or forthrightness. As the whole picture is chaotic, you have to open to the chaos before you can be open to the calm.

This time of Earth changes is a revolutionary time. No matter how bad or difficult it may seem, it should be accepted as the grace of the Great Mother, so hold to your center and persevere. For now, you don't have to dive that deeply into the ocean to cross it, because the ocean is opening up to meet you.

Instinctual-Self

Opening up to instinctual-self is like opening up Pandora's box. It seems scary, for we never know what will come out. In that place of unknowing, you must make an additional leap of faith into your higher self, so that your intelligent will can allow your instinctual-self to open and reveal itself. The dark energy reminds you of your animal nature and the need to survive. For you to have peace within your being, however, this energy must be purified, its gross vibrations must be released and your energy transformed. At times, as a frightened child, you felt this same energy of apprehension on those scary nights. Now open to it, release it to higher self, and be free. Stay open until it is completely gone, until you are completely empty. If necessary, repeat this meditation over and over again until you are free. When you release that part of you that you perceive as a beast, what remains is your self as child.

Conscience

Conscience is a little tricky to deal with, because it is tied to ego or personality-self as it passes its judgment on shadow and instinctual-self. The trick is to understand that ego or personality-self can't transform conscience. This needs to be done from the place of "I Am," or higher self. As higher self takes over, conscience begins to fade away, leaving higher self to balance your emotions and bring you into the flow of the Great Mother and the place of the co-creator with spirit. This has to be a conscious opening up and letting go to bring the things that are in the darkness into the light. They must be released so you can heal. One might say, "It's a painful process," but one has to open up to the pain and release the pain in order to heal and begin to experience the joy.

Relationships

This time of the dark night of the soul is especially impor-tant because it can bring about the end of a close personal relationship. It is at this time that you have to reflect long and hard about the relationship, without being judgmental. You have to ask the question, "What can I learn from this? Is this a lesson from the Great Mother? Is there more I need to learn or understand about getting into a positive, longlasting relationship? Or, is it just the Creator's way of telling me it's time to move on?" You have to be clear about this. If you ask the Great Mother, she will help you become clear about your life direction. This may mark a turning point in your spiritual life, a time of test, when you are given a chance to increase your level of commitment to spiritual life and higher self, to see whether you are willing to stand alone in partnership with the Creator, as co-creator. Then, if you continue to work in close personal relationship with another, it will be the Creator's will, not your own. You may feel, however, that you are still looking for a soulmate to complete your life's expression, so you need to be very clear about how you should proceed. It is a time when men and women of light will stop living in the shadows, and come into the light. It is a time of great suffering, upheaval, and change.

Transformation

In living through the process of transformation you must, at some point, open up to those so-called negative things that have been happening in your life and re-examine them

with new eyes. Now you understand they are there because of you. They have come into your reality because
you are you. So search inside yourself to find out what
part of yourself may be pulling in this negativity. It may
be an unconscious attitude or way of being. It may be
triggered from an unconscious resentment from some past
experiences buried deep in your subconscious. It could be
karma from a past lifetime. Or some reaction you experience trying to bring the instinctual part of your nature
into balance. Or freeing the scared, frightened child trapped
inside your instinctual-self. In the process of transformation, you have to give every part of yourself a voice and
develop the ability to clearly distinguish between the internal voices of each part of yourself—to discern the difference between intellect (your conscious mind) and how
it balances with soul (your subconscious mind); to distinguish between your conscience and your "I Am," or superconscious mind and how it balances your emotions, with
its passions and appetites. You must then engage your intelligent will to open up the instinctual-self with its feelings and drives. Shine the light of consciousness on the
yin energy of the Great Mother within, so that it counter
balances the yang energy of spirit—Father. With the aide
of the Great Mother and higher self, you begin to open to
the shadow or yin side of your being. Then you can face
and acknowledge the shadow side of yourself. When you

do this, you gain the capacity to step beyond the wall of the subconscious mind, by bringing all parts of self into consciousness. Then you are able to face the demons of the subconscious without fear. Then you can acknowledge who or what they are and gain an understanding of how you can best deal with them, bringing all parts of self into balance. In living through this process, your spiritual life may, for a while, seem kind of hellish, as you integrate the shadow side of your being. In the process of transformation, strong vibrational energies are released as you begin to go through the clearing process. Those living near you may chide you or harass you for the gross quality of the vibrational energy. You must realize that this vibrational energy has been building up inside you ever since childhood. There is no need to feel you have to justify yourself or explain why you have this gross energy. They probably wouldn't understand anyway. With the release of the gross vibrational energy, the remaining spiritual energy will be answer enough. You'll find that even things from past lifetimes will surface and come forth into your life. When you live through a seemingly negative experience in a positive way, you transform the nature of the energy, and it can no longer intimidate you. Since yin and yang are two parts of the reality before you, as you become aware of the positive spiritual yang energy around you, you also automatically become aware of the negative or opposite yin energies in your reality. Now you don't have to be afraid of the phantoms that come by night and try to cast shadows on your days, for you know they are but reflections of your opposite or shadow side. They represent the internal wall that you have come to. Instead of seeing the phantoms as negative obstructions facing you, now see them as the shadow side of yourself that they are. You can step beyond them by integrating them into your reality, for you understand that all things are part of the Tao. In the realm of yin/yang, we give power to negativity by acknowledging its existence as negative to us.

In 1958, the spiritual master Meher Baba held a gathering of his close followers in Myrtle Beach, South Carolina, which he called his *Sahavas*—the master giving his association to the close Baba lovers. In one of his discourses at the gathering (as I can best remember), he spoke with hand gestures to one of his *mandali* (who interpreted) of good and evil, and how we give power to evil by considering it the opposite of good. He used the example of a string. One end he called good, the other end he called evil. Then he went to a point midway between the ends and asked, "Is this point good or evil?" He said it is dependent on your point of reference, how you judge it— moderately good, or moderately evil. Then he moved the reference point in increments toward the side of good and asked, "What is this?" Then he moved the reference point to the side of evil and asked, "Now what is this"? With this, it became clear that everything was relative to the end points. He said if that is so, that all points on the string are relative to the end points, why don't we call one of the end points good, and the other end point the furthest extension of good? Then every point along the string is a different degree of good.

So, we can turn the negative energy in our lives by acknowledging it as just the furthest extension of what we perceive as positive and good, and accepting it as a part of our reality. We have to be able to deal with fear before we can truly be open to love. The realization here represents a paradigm shift, for, from the place of soul, we realize that the demons that attack us by night and cast their shadows on our days are no more than reflections from our own shadow side. We may find they are also projected onto others in the world around us. But we can, with the help of the Great Mother and higher self, begin to deal with the demons on the inside, for we can see them as the walls of obstruction within us. The obstruction represents all those things you were ever afraid of in your life, from childhood to the present, and all those people and situations that they are projected onto in the world around you. As you view them as the furthest or subconscious extension of your reality, your vision begins to shift and you see them on another level, as extensions of your self, for, on the soul level, we are all part of the human family and we are all connected. Then you manifest the clearing by acknowledging that they have a right to their existence, just as you have a right to yours. By doing this, you simply acknowledge the place that they have in the overall scheme of life. It also means you are standing in the place of soul and acknowledging your "I Am" as spirit, your true self, and manifesting your right to be. Living by the Universal Law, you do not infringe on them, so you are not infringed on by them. They are free to live their lives as they choose; you are free to live your life as you choose. As you extend the energy of compassion to them, you begin to feel the connection, and this opens your heart up to compassion for them—and also for yourself—to wake you up from the illusion. As the obstruction begins to clear, the walls begin to melt away.

You may need to go through this clearing process a number of times before the obstruction is sufficiently cleared away on the inside, for you to feel fully free on the outside. In the way of transformation, you have to go on until all the programs are played out before true change is possible. You have to let your shadow and instinctual-self join in with the other parts of self to get rid of all of the old programs. Until you do, complete change is not possible, because you haven't gotten at the root cause of your obstruction, which are the dissonant programs. The obstruction could be from shadow or instinctual-self, or it could be reflected onto the emotional level. Until you are open enough and honest enough with yourself to allow the dissonant programs to play out and the root cause of the disruptive energy to surface and show itself, you will not be able to complete the process of transformation.

The root cause of this disruptive energy lies hidden in the dark recesses of your subconscious, growing, festering, and triggering your emotions, and instigating your reactions from a place beyond the surface of your consciousness. When this part of self has its full say, you will become aware of where the subconscious hook is—the source of the discordant energy vibrations, from the imbalanced place you find yourself in. For the first time, the feelings and emotions from the deepest parts of yourself will have a chance to show themselves for what they are. Release the lust, hate, and pent-up anger with others, with life, with God. Give your own demons a chance to show themselves. Acknowledge them, and then release them. It is only in performing this final step in the process that the healing can be complete. You have to release the gross attachments of lust, of hate, the discordant feelings of anger, of insufficiency, of selfishness, and become empty. Then you will be free to love, to start all over again. Your inside and outside have to become one. You need to clear your internal channels so, when you go inside for guidance from the

Great Mother, and higher self, it will not be influenced by stored anger and resentment, or dissonant feelings from past experiences. This disruptive energy is still stored in the subconscious as vibrations and will color your innermost thoughts and feelings.

Vow to rid yourself of all the dissonant programs within your being, then push on until you begin to dislodge them from the hidden recesses deep within your being. Know that this disruptive energy vibration is there. It represents the dust or dirt that is covering the mirror of your heart, clouding your vision so that you cannot see clearly. Without fear or apprehension, allow this dissonant energy vibration to surface and show itself. Acknowledge it, then do whatever is necessary to deal with it.

As love and forgiveness now transform the original pain in your heart, you open up to compassion. And remember, working with the energy of compassion, rather than anger or resentment, gives others the space and the opportunity to change, to be more, to become free of the illusion. Once this is done, you become a clear, transparent medium, like an unclouded mirror that reflects the true nature of your soul's being. You become whole as soul, as symbolized by the circle. This state is called Crystal Purity.

This is where you move from the position of just trying to maintain harmony in your life to the place of balance. As your reality shifts, you are able to be open to both sides without the need to judge. You are able to find balance within imbalance, imbalance within balance, and still hold your center. You are able to be open to both the positive and negative experiences within your reality and still feel free to be.

Coming into the Age of Aquarius, as the energies of the Great Mother increase, you may find it increasingly difficult to maintain a harmonious existence. The old forces of inertia are resistant to change. This cannot be, however, for the Earth is going through regeneration and the old energies must give way to the new. When they do not, the energies act upon one another to create a critical point where change must occur, either internally or externally, to avert a crisis. Although here we are talking about internal change, you will increasingly begin to see the need to live through the change externally as well, because the crisis will also take place externally. To avoid the fear and chaos, and to bring about positive change, you must circumvent the external chaos by acknowledging it as a manifestation or a reflection of the chaos within. Through prayer and meditation, send love and light into the situation and a realization will come. You will gain a clear understanding of the meaning for this chaos in your life, as well as the need to live through this chaos in a positive way. By allowing each part of the chaos to be, without being judgmental, you also develop and manifest the capacity to be.

Those who live through this experience in a positive way will become free of the chaos in their lives and come in tune with the will of the Creator as higher self. They will become open to the realm of Tai Chi, where love and enlightened consciousness meet as intuition. They will also realize that this is but a stepping-stone to the next phase, the second step into the Way, the opening up to spirit that is given by the grace of spirit.

Now you can realize the importance of incorporating the shadow side and the light side in order to become whole. As the shadow recedes, your heart becomes open to compassion, and, after all, it is love plus wisdom that gives compassion. This is the energy needed to see you through the Earth changes. Your willingness to join with and work in harmony with the Great Mother and the Creator as higher self will help facilitate the transformation of the planet and all that are on it.

17

Taoist Thirty-Three Energies & The Thirty-Six Energies of Creation

The idea of thirty-two basic energies (with Earth making the thirty-third) is not something unique to the Taoist tradition. It is simply an understanding of some of the energy vibrations that we experience in the material plane. From the *I Ching,* the Chinese Book of Changes, we take the Pa Qua, which portrays eight dynamic energy cycles that manifest in the material world. Each of these eight energies becomes a part of one of the four elements. The element of wood (or nature), the element of fire, the element of metal (or air), and the element of water all form a different Pa Qua, with Earth as the central element. This creates thirty-three energy vibrations within the physical dimension.

The energy of infinity is an energy vibration of the Tao, or Spirit, from the source. The energy of quest is a vibration of the Great Mother, and it's one of the thirty-three energies in this dimension. When you quest, you begin to extend yourself into other dimensions, such as the spiritual dimension, and you find there are more energies than you can count. The thirty-three energies apply only to the physical dimension. If you come to an understanding of the thirty-three energies, or come into a positive relationship with the Great Mother, you, in essence, can transcend the physical dimension and open to the dimension that is called Tai Chi.

In Tai Chi, you no longer vibrate with the energies of the physical dimension, or yin/yang). You start to create your own energies. In other words, these physical energies have no further meaning for you. In Tai Chi, you become an initiate, and as an initiate, you transcend the physical dimension. You become transformed by the Great Mother's energy thirty-three, the highest energy in the material world. As you pass or transcend the physical dimension, you become, in essence, whole within yourself, or soul.

The next initiation occurs when soul comes into union with spirit—the "I Am," the yang energy of the Father, energy thirty-four. This energy brings you into the yang side of the realm of Tai Chi and brings about a balancing of yin and yang energies within your being.

Then you come into the energy we call Wu Chi, or Lo Gay—energy thirty-five. Wu Chi is a great cycle of which our creation is a part. The energy here is no longer the energy of the initiate, for there is no individual existence here. You become a part of the creation and, at the same time, you are, in essence, non-existent.

Finally, you come to energy thirty-six, which is another dimension we call *Wheh*, emptiness, or void, that is talked about by the Taoist Chuang Tzu. Void is the last energy of our creation. This combines and completes the circle of the thirty-six levels of energy.

Of course, from a Taoist religious perspective, there are thirty-six levels of heaven, which means there are thirty-six levels of energy to which we can attune ourselves and of which we can become a part. This, in essence, presents the thirty-six energies in a physical sense, so that you can relate to them more easily.

Now, existence is a massive energy that seeks little units of energy through which to express itself. You may call this energy God, you may call it the Great Spirit, you may call it Tao, or you may call it Universal Mind. Whatever it is, it is an all-powerful thing, and because it is all-powerful, it is in all things. It does not manipulate. It is infinity within infinity. This infinite mind, this Universal Mind, created an energy source we call humanity. So humanity, in essence, contains everything that's in the physical, because that energy source needed something through which to express itself in the physical. Man stands within the physical plane giving balance to all things. He, in essence, is all things, but because he is yang to the Great Mother's yin, he loses the balance within himself and finds himself imbalanced within the physical plane. As a woman's nature is yin and harmonious with the Great Mother, it's easier for her to maintain her balance in the physical. Man's nature is thus a structure he has to build upon. Once he begins to build upon the structure of his energy, he can actually experience union as soul with the Great Soul, or the Great Mother's energy thirty-three. This opens the way to a more complete structure of man's energy, which, in the West, is called the "I Am." As a woman comes in tune with her nature, energy thirty-three of the Great Mother, she can become open to yang energy directly as her "I Am." The "I Am" is not the higher self, nor is it the soul or the Great Soul. It is a definitive (smallest, but original) part of the source of this infinite energy. This means the "I Am" that you perceive within yourself (in Sanskrit called *jivatma*, or individualized spirit-soul) is a definitive (smallest, but original) aspect of spirit. This allows you to open to and express this infinite energy. The "I Am" is the enlightened mind, if you want to use the mind; but the "I Am" is also the bridge that connects you with the higher self. It's the bridge that connects you with the Universal

Mind that we call infinity, that we call Tao. If the infinite power is in all things, that means you express yourself through what it is. That's why we have to be here, because this allows the God force a chance to feel and express itself, within itself. Because we are all part of the God force, we feel it and express it within our selves, which in essence, allows the God force to feel itself. This means we, in essence, become a part of what that is—just as, in Christianity, it is said God made man in his image. Does that mean God looks like a man? No, nor does it mean that man looks like God. God made man in his image. God is holy, so we are meant to be holy. We have the God force within us. The Tao is always there, but it needs something to allow it to materialize, to allow it to express itself. How does the God force do this? By allowing a gap in the structure of our energy (as soul) that can be bridged by the "I Am," the enlightened mind (as spirit). This will connect the God force with whatever we are utilizing to express ourselves in the world. The "I Am" thus becomes the bridge of the enlightened mind that we can use to express everything in a broader, more complete way. Your "I Am" is a personal "I Am." But it's also a definitive "I Am" beyond your body. It is the fullness that you can be.

Figure 12 (page 216) shows that the four elements in the material realm have become a part of the eight energies of the Pa Qua, creating four Pa Qua of thirty-two

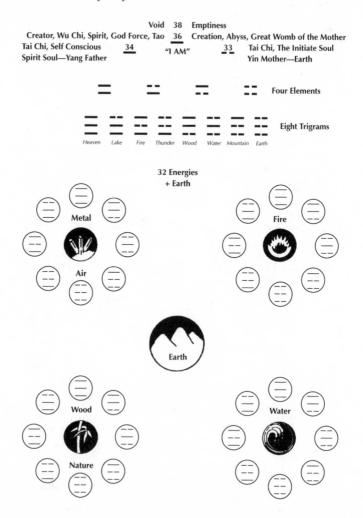

Figure 12. The Four Elements in the Western System.

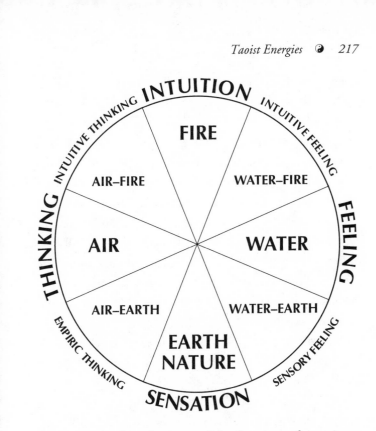

Figure 13. The four elements and the functions of consciousness. If you are working with the Western system of the four elements, representing the four temperaments of man, you have metal (or air) opposite water, and fire opposite wood (or nature). Earth is not generally included as an element in the Western System, but you can include it into your life by opening to it as Earth Mother, or, if you prefer, as the Goddess, the Great Mother, or the feminine principle representing the miracle of the birth of all life on the planet—in all its forms.

energies, with Earth located centrally as energy thirty-three. Energy thirty-three is also the yin energy of the Great Mother in the realm of Tai Chi. If you work with the Western system used by Jung and others, you work with the four temperaments (see figure 13, page 217). To this is added the fifth element, Earth, symbolized as Earth Mother, or the Great Mother in Her many aspects: the Goddess, the Great Soul, or the Terrible Mother. As the Terrible Mother, she represents those things you still have to balance on the shadow side. It is through coming into a positive relationship with the Great Mother as the transformational energy of Quest (energy thirty-three) that your way becomes open.

Figure 14 (page 220) shows that the four elements in the subtle realm have merged with the eight energies of the Pa Qua to form thirty-two energies around Earth, energy thirty-three in the material realm. In the Chinese system, the energy of Earth is represented as the fifth element of their Five-Element Theory (see figure 15, page 221). Energy thirty-three also represents the energy of Quest, the spiritual energy of the Great Mother in the realm of Tai Chi.

The yang energy of the Father is energy thirty-four. This energy represents the initiate of the Father, the self as conscious spirit-soul. Here you become open to the yang energy of the Father. This energy of the Father is not just a realization of consciousness. It is a balancing of the energy of the Great Mother, creating, as the Taoist say, a sage baby within your being. This is your realization of self as spirit-soul. This is the realization that allows higher self to utilize you as a bridge or an instrument to express itself in the world. If man goes to the yang energy (thirty-four) without first becoming balanced by the energy (thirty-three) of the Great Mother, although he will have a realization of consciousness, his being nature will still be entangled in yin/yang, the material world.

Energy thirty-five—Wu Chi or Lo Gay—represents the energy of this creation. It is the great cycle in which all life forms play a part. It is the source of this creation. You tune into this realm of being as part of yourself, and into the experience of what lies beyond. The energy thirty-six represents a doorway into the next dimension, one beyond the material universe. It is the energy of emptiness, of void.

Yin and Yang—
The Dual Nature of the Divine

In a sense, the Creator has two hands just as we do. The Creator's left hand is the feminine energy of the Great Mother, which we called the Tao of yin. The Creator's right hand is the masculine energy of the Father or the Creator, which we called the Tao of yang. In periods of trial and

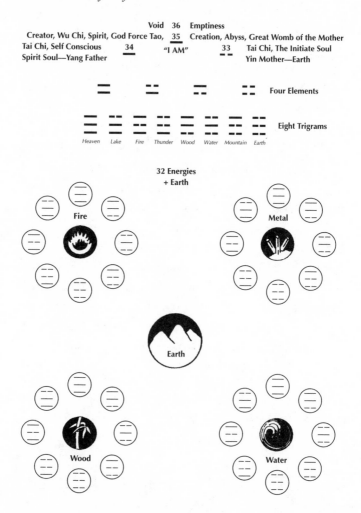

Figure 14. The four elements plus Earth in the Chinese system.

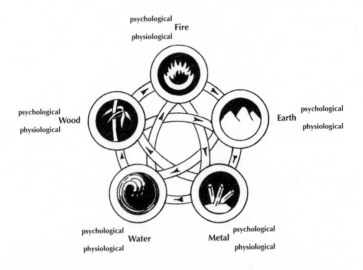

Figure 15. The pattern of five-phase relationship. If you are working with the Chinese system of the four elements with Earth representing the fifth element, you have the pattern of the five-phase relationship, or the Five-Element Theory. Earth takes its place as the fifth element in conjunction with the other four elements, to help bring the balance of Earth Mother into everyday life. The Five-Element Theory forms the basis for Chinese medicine—bringing balance to imbalances within the body and in the world. You can work with the five archetypes and do an assessment of yourself on a physiological and psychological level to determine your type, and determine how best to bring yourself into balance. For more information on the five-phase relationship of Chinese medicine, or the Five-Element Theory, refer to *Between Heaven and Earth*, by Harriet Beinfield. (Figure redrawn from two illustrations from *Between Heaven and Earth* (New York: Ballantine Books, 1991), p. 96, 154.

test, as in the dark of night, it may seem as though even God is against us. If you remain firm, however, and don't deviate from your connection to and reliance on the Creator, you will find your way. If it is God the Father who is trying you and you call on God the Mother for help, She will soon come to your rescue. Likewise, when you are besieged by the Great Mother, you can, with prayer, meditation, and mantras, tune into the energy of the Father to help you through the difficult times. It is not as though the divine wants you to fail, although sometimes it may seem like that. At those times, instead of turning against God the Mother or God the Father, you should turn to the other aspect of the divine energy for help. In that way, you can remain positively linked to the divine in what may seem to be a very negative situation.

When you relate to the Tao as the One, creative energy of the Creator, as Universal Mind, you view it as an impersonal energy. The Tao only cares because you care. When you care about your life and spiritual energy, you can attract it to you. Then you begin to interact with the Tao. You begin to perceive that it consists of two aspects—yin and yang. You come to realize that the Tao of yin counterbalances the Tao of yang, and is manifesting in the realm of yin/yang. The Tao is not limited to the spiritual realm, but manifests in the world around you. Therefore, you can become open to the mercy of the Tao of yin, which is the grace of the Great Mother, the Tao in the here and now.

When you begin to differentiate between the two aspects of the Tao, it ceases to be impersonal and begins to take on personal attributes, according to your preconceived or perceived relationship with the divine. It is at this point that your previous connections with deity, or your newfound connection with deity, can bring new light into your life, and open a new dimension into the realm of yin/yang. You begin to realize that these energies of the deities are to be realized inside and not outside your self. We are spirit-souls, and they are within our beings. They are within all people, and within all creation.

When you become whole, as soul, you regain the memory of your past lives. This realization takes you past the narrow attachment to race, gender, and creed. It brings you into a place of wholeness, of feeling one with all others, because you've been there.

To Be Free

In order to be free enough to be, to be able to deal with the walls of obstruction around and within you, it would be advantageous for you to take the shelter of the Great Mother. Since the Creator does everything, it would be naive of you to ask the Creator to stop doing the things that are causing your obstruction, without first seeking to find out if there is something you need to learn from these things. Understand clearly, if there are lessons the Creator wants you to learn in life, you can't move on until you learn them. You have to open up to all of life's experiences as part of your growing process in the school of life. But you can beseech the Great Mother to become your ally. That is how you can cross the ocean of Maya to higher ground. When she is your ally, you can safely step into her space without fear of being destroyed. Better than that, you feel she is giving you shelter, that she is your guardian, and guide, opening the way for you.

The Earth is Our Mother

As you begin to become whole, you gain the realization that the Earth is indeed your mother. You are born on her; you dwell on her, and take your shelter from her. You get your sustenance from her. When you are sick, you get your medicine from her. As you become more mature and open to spirit, you find that it is Earth Mother that nurtures your soul. As the soul is the vibrating energy coming from spirit that inundates your body, it establishes your state of being. The soul can become contaminated by coming into contact with disruptive energy vibrations. The Great Mother as Earth Mother comes to your rescue by graciously receiving the toxic vibrations that have polluted your soul's energy and healing you with a soothing balm. Indeed, as you walk through life's valleys, she restores your soul. By uniting with her, you become open to the Great Mother as your guardian, your guide into the next dimension as spirit.

Divine Law and You

When you stop consciously working with divine law because divine law is working with you, you know you are doing the Creator's will and not your own. You come into the place of co-creator when you understand that the divine is behind all the changes that life is putting you through for your soul's good. In the same way, you come to realize that the divine is behind all of life's changes, for the good of all. When you understand this enough to let all other souls be, you can be also.

A strange thing happens when you begin to do this. You start to perceive the divine in all those around you. When you perceive the divine in all those around you, the divine makes your heart sing. For then, you understand and you come to know that you and the divine are not two, but one.

18

The Eight Taoist Immortals[19]

Taoism has come down to us from ancient times with a focus on being in harmony with nature. Its roots are in shamanism. Although there are many schools of Taoism, there are two main branches. Tao Chia—the school of the Way—is the philosophical form of Taoism. This is the form best known in the West from Lao Tzu's classic *Tao Te Ching*. Tao Chiao, which means "the religion of the Way," is present wherever Chinese live. Tao, of course, means Way,

---

[19] For more information on the Eight Taoist Immortals, see *The Eight Immortals of Taoism: Legends and Fables of Popular Taoism*, translated and edited by Kwok Man Ho and Joanne O'Brien, with Introduction by Martin Palmer (New York: Penguin, 1990). The text on the Tao and the Eight Immortals that follows is paraphrased from that source. The drawings are my own.

path, or way to truth. Being in harmony with the universal laws and the fundamental natural forces or energies of creation is following the natural way.

Although there is a span of several centuries between the times when the Eight Taoist Immortals lived, there are stories of the Eight Immortals walking down a country road as they engaged in their pastimes together. These stories indicate the persistence of the legend of their longevity. The important thing for us, however, is not so much how long the Immortals lived, but the quality of life they lived through their pastimes. By their lives, they show us how to transcend yin/yang. This is achieved not so much by eating a peach of immortality, or taking a pill of immortality, but by following in their footsteps in our daily lives. Each of the Eight Immortals has his or her own particular personality, and his or her own energy. It is up to those who choose to follow the way of the Eight Immortals to find out how they relate to each of the Immortals' energies. These energies represent the eight basic energies of the Pa Qua (see figure 17, page 242) that, when combined, bring us into the One. When all parts of ourselves, or all seven chakras, are working and balanced harmoniously with the eighth, all eight begin to function as one. The eighth chakra, above the head, becomes the first chakra in a new octave or dimension we call Tai Chi. In the same way, even though all of the Eight Immortals have their own temperaments and personalities, because they are balanced and living harmoniously within themselves and within the group, they each function from the One, in his or her own way. Or the One functions through each of them—simultaneously one, but different.

Lu Tung Pin

Of the Eight Immortals, Lu Tung Pin is the most popular. It is said that Lu Tung Pin is the easiest of the Immortals to contact because of his concern for the welfare of his worshippers. Statues dedicated to him can be found in most temples in towns and villages and many grottoes on the sacred mountains of China.

Lu Tung Pin is considered the doctor of the poor. If you are ill and not sure exactly what to do, you can visit one of Lu Tung Pin's shrines. After sincere prayers, describe your symptoms and then shake the container holding the numbered bamboo sticks, each representing an energy associated with a different medical condition. When one falls, note the number and bring it to the prescription shop or the priest to get a prescription to take to the herbalist. Lu Tung Pin's symbol is a large sword that he is usually shown carrying.

The sword is known as the Devil Slayer. It is believed that if he is invoked correctly, through charms, he will use his sword to tame or capture evil spirits. He is represented as the sorcerer, the magician, the shaman.

Ti Kuai Li

The next most popular character is Ti Kuai Li. Because of his association with medicine, the sign of his iron crutch often hangs outside apothecary shops. He's not as popular as Lu Tung Pin because of his eccentricities and well-known bad temper. Although he is a doctor and can provide prescriptions, these are not usually sought by the devout unless there is a Taoist priest in the area who has some connection with him.

Professional exorcists favor him for his magical medical gourd, his other sign. Ti Kuai Li's popularity derives from his unpredictable and vexatious character. Through no choice of his own, he has the form of a beggar, which he uses to fight for the rights of the poor and downtrodden. He is very much the clown figure, whose popularity is based upon being seen as a beggar who is a testy clown. He is more powerful, however, than his strongest adversary. He's represented as the teacher, the healer, the medicine man.

Chang Kuo Lau

Chang Kuo Lau is usually pictured riding his donkey, often riding the poor creature backwards. He carries a strange musical instrument in his hand—a long bamboo tube with smaller tubes emerging from the top. Chang Kuo Lau's picture is often found hanging above bridal beds or in the homes of young couples, or couples desiring to have children. For some reason buried in the past, Chang Kuo Lau is seen as the bringer of offspring, especially boys. Because of this, he is figured on  many calendars produced in the Chinese world and is invoked by worried families. He is represented as the keeper of the archives, the knower of antiquity, the sage.

Tsao Kuo Chiu

Tsao Kuo Chiu was the brother of the Queen, a member of the imperial court, and a dangerous man to cross. His promotion to the rank of Immortal appears more like an

act of caprice by the other seven, who wished to fill the eighth cave on their mountain. He was a most unlikely choice for immortality. He was a reformed murderer who, it seems, looked useful, so he was made an immortal. He has the ability to clearly discern if one is functioning from one's lower self or higher self (see "A Teaching from Tsao Kuo Chiu" on page 234).

Ts'ao Kuo Chiu being chosen for immortality is an indication that we all have a chance for transformation. His symbols are an imperial tablet of recommendation, or a pair of castanets. He seems to have attracted little devotion down the centuries. He represents the world server, the affluent official, the achiever.

Han Hsiang Tzu

Han Hsiang Tzu is traditionally seen as the patron of musicians. He is much loved and his symbol is a beautiful jade flute. He is a great poet and musician, a lover of the solitude and beauty of the mountains. He represents the ideal of a truly contented person, dwelling in the harmony of the universe in bliss, with true appreciation of the beauty of its solitary places. He is depicted as a true Taoist mountain man. He represents the artist, the poet, the musician.

Han Chung Li

Han Chung Li lived during the Han dynasty. He is a fascinating historical figure who rose high in the imperial service. There are stories in which he is portrayed as a general or a field marshal. There are other stories that portray him as a provincial governor. He is famous for inventing the alchemical pill of immortality and is a popular figure for those seeking longevity. His symbol is a feathery fan held in his left hand, or sometimes he carries the peach of immortality. He represents the hero, the general, the leader.

Lan Ts'ai Ho

Lan Ts'ai Ho is portrayed at times as female, at times as male. He is the strangest of all the Immortals. He rep-

resents the jester, the unbalanced one, a figure recognized and usually handled better in older societies, where it was believed that such people were touched by God or the gods. He is not worshipped for himself and it is not known why he holds a basket of flowers, other than for collecting and enjoying all possible varieties. He represents the conjurer, the eternal child, the god-touched.

Ho Hsien Ku

Ho Hsien Ku is the only woman in the group (although occasionally Lan Ts'ai Ho is depicted as a woman). That there is a woman in this group at all is most surprising, for there is no tradition of female ascetics in Tao Chia and few senior female practitioners of Tao Chiao. She brings the energy of the Great Mother into the Pa Qua, and provides the nurturing energy of yin to balance the creative energy of yang. Ho Hsien Ku provides a way for seekers to connect with the Great Mother and receive her nurtur-

ing and protection. She was granted immortality because of her ascetic practices. She is recognized by her lotus flower symbol, meaning openness and wisdom. She is not venerated for her own sake. She represents the mystic female, the wise woman, Earth Mother who is the nurturer.

A Teaching from Tsao Kuo Chiu

To give you a better insight into Tsao Kuo Chiu, I will relate a story given to me at a Taoist temple, in response to a hexagram I received from the *I Ching*. It was in answer to a question I had asked about how to make positive change in my life. The story was about the twin sons of the ruler of a small kingdom. While they were still quite young, the ruler passed away, leaving the kingdom to his sons. One son had the qualities of sincere regard and compassion for the people of the kingdom and he was chosen to rule. The other son was envious of his brother's good fortune and decided to make it his own. He locked his brother away in a secret room inside the castle so no one could find him. He said his brother left on a journey and he didn't know when he would return, and so he was coronated king in his place.

Then the kingdom fell on hard times, with extravagant living, and sending of warring expeditions into the neighboring kingdoms. With severe droughts, the crops failed and the treasury became depleted, leaving the burden of carrying the kingdom on the people with heavy taxation. With this, the people longed for the brother who was the rightful ruler to return, for he would surely know what to do to change their fate.

Things got so bad that the twin brother who was the present ruler turned to his imprisoned brother for help. The imprisoned brother told him he would gladly take over the responsibility for the situation if his twin brother would take his place in the secret room. The twin brother agreed, so the rightful twin took over the reign of the country. In a very short time, he brought the warring campaigns to an end, and the young men returned to their homes to help harvest the bountiful crops. With the ruling class returning to sensible living, he began to restore the treasury and lift the heavy burden of taxation from the backs of the people. Prosperity began to shine on the small kingdom once again. The people gave thanks to the Creator that the wrong had been made right.

This was a teaching from Tsao Kuo Chiu. In this hexagram, he is saying, stop being the victim. Allow your true self to come alive, come out of the enclosure within yourself and take your rightful place as the ruler of your life. Take the responsibility for your life and step into the place of co-creator of your reality.

The Eight Taoist Immortals and the Eight Trigrams of the Pa Qua

Most Westerners have never heard of the Eight Taoist Immortals. For those who have, they are simply the subjects of some good stories, but they do not play a serious role in Western lives. This presentation of the Eight Taoist Immortals is intended to show their relationship to the transformational use of the eight trigrams of the Pa Qua. The Eight Taoist Immortals relate to the eight subtle or transcendental energies of the universe. These eight subtle or transcendental energies are also represented by the eight trigrams of the Pa Qua. Coming into positive relationship with the Eight Taoist Immortals is a wonderful way to bring positive change and transformation into your life. The Eight Taoist Immortals are eight Chinese saints, a manifestation of the eight subtle energies of the eight trigrams. As we said before, the eight trigrams are the basis of the *I Ching*, China's most ancient book of divination. They also form the foundation of *feng shui*—Chinese geomancy. Each of the

Eight Taoist Immortals is associated with one of the eight trigram directions.

The Place or Seat of Transformation

The importance of the saints or Immortals, the deities or masters, is that they help us focus on or tune in to spiritual energy. It is the energy that takes us to the quiet place inside ourselves. Some chant sacred names, some focus on the sacred image of the saints or deities, some sing sacred songs, dance, and play the sacred drum. In this presentation of the Way of the Tao, we use the Pa Qua as a focus on the eight subtle energies associated with the saints or Immortals that represent the eight subtle energies in nature, in the world, and inside ourselves. We bring these energies into balance as we focus on that still place within our own hearts that's linked to the quiet place of "I Am" within our minds. When we go there, time seemingly stands still and we feel at peace. This is the place we come to for help, for guidance, for shelter and nurturing. When we incorporate the guidance and realizations we get from the saints, or Immortals, deities, or masters from this quiet place into every aspect of our daily lives, we spark the internal processes of self-integration and self-transformation to take place within ourselves.

19

Create Your Own Mandala

Joseph Campbell spoke on the Public Broadcast System program, *The Power of Myth with Bill Moyers*, and Bill Moyers asked him about the circle as being a universal symbol or mandala. Joseph Campbell said, "In working out a mandala for oneself, what one does is draw a circle and then think of the different impulse systems in your life, the different value systems in your life, and try then to compose them and find what the center is. It's a kind of discipline for pulling all those scattered aspects of your life together."

When you walk the Way of the Tao, you do not manifest the true Tao directly. Rather, you open out to the eight subtle energies of the Pa Qua that were first conceived in the mind of the Creator in Wu Chi or Jade Purity, and manifested in the mind-body of the gods or divine beings of Tai Chi or Crystal Purity. The Pa Qua represents the eight basic or subtle energies of this universe. It is from these eight subtle energies that the material world of yin/yang manifests.

In order to make the journey home, you must resolve your life changes sufficiently to stand in the place of the eight subtle energies of Tai Chi. You can do this by creating your own mandala of the eight subtle energies. They represent the eight aspects of yourself in the mind-body of the Creator.

The Way becomes open when your ego or personality-self and soul join in positive relationship with the Great Soul and with spirit as your higher self. It is, therefore, necessary to understand that you are energy and that all things are energy. As you are one with this energy, you are one with all things. You are linked to the source through this energy, called the Tao, or Spirit. You can personalize the Tao and call on it as spirit, Father, Buddha, Krishna, Yaweh, Jehovah, JA, Allah, Olodumare, Wakananda, or the divine name according to your path. You can call on it as the Great Soul or the Great Mother in her many aspects: as Shekhinah or the Holy Ghost, the Goddess, the Mystic Female, or the divine name according to your path. Or you can leave it impersonal, as the God force that is both Father and Mother in one, the Universal Mind or energy that is the source of all creation. Whether you relate to the Creator in the impersonal aspect or in the personal aspect as the source of all energy, that energy is found within your own being and not outside anywhere. You can open up internally to the God force, the Tao, that energy that is the livingness within you that links you with the livingness in all things.

As you step into the magic circle of the mandala, reflect on the transcendental representation that you choose to represent each aspect of yourself. Then visualize how they bring each aspect of yourself together to live in the One.

Figure 16 (see page 241) shows an interfaith mandala. Each line should reflect an area in your life that is important to you. I have placed some Hindu deities in one circle on the mandala, and some Christian saints on another circle, as well as a circle containing Yoruba Orishas, and another containing eight planets. Together they form the Interfaith Pa Qua of the Open Door. As you reflect on this mandala, concentrate on the nature of the energy of each of the eight centers. The Pa Qua, or mandala, that you create must represent you, for your highest good, so choose well and use your power to manifest your own reality.

On the circle of the mandala with the Hindu deities, the Goddesses Durga and Kali are represented in the second place, the instinctual center, opposite the God

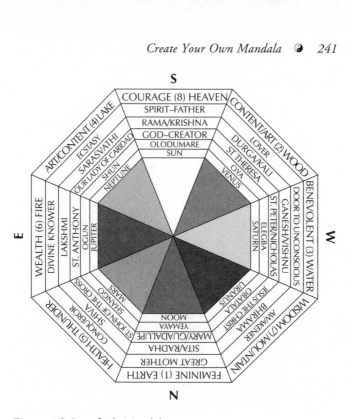

Figure 16. Interfaith Mandala.

Shiva in the fifth place, the place of will. When Durga's energy is present in this center, it represents the place of contentment, for those who want to live a happy family life. However, in the process of transforming the energy of the instinctual center, the energy makes a

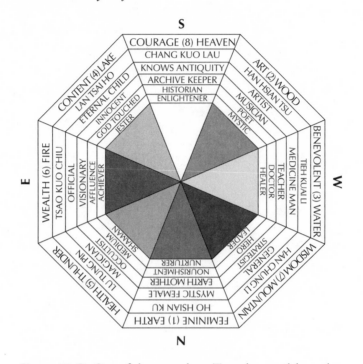

Figure 17. Pa Qua of the open door. Turn the mandala so that you are facing the aspect or energy that you are working with.

---

fundamental shift and you experience a world-weariness. At this point, Kali's energy can be perceived working with you for the transformation of your instinctual-self. This makes for the mystic, the poet, the artist and musician, the seeker.

Goddess Sarasvati is in the fourth place, the place of art. Here you find the artists and musicians represented under Sarasvati. In the process of transformation, she functions internally as the Muse, so that, through your art, you experience ecstasy, making this center the place of contentment. There is a subtle shift in the energies of the second and fourth place.

In figure 17 (page 242), the Pa Qua of the Open Door, the transformational shift to the energy of quest is seen with Han Hsiang Tzu in the second place, representing Art, and Lan Tsai Ho in the fourth place, representing contentment. It was difficult, at first, to realize why the Pa Qua took this form, but a closer look at the deities of the Hindu circle provides insight on this.

Figures 2, 3, 11, 16, and 17 can help you get started making your mandala (see pp. 11, 140, 191, 241, and 242). Enter the six lines to your mandala (figure 19) that you feel will help you get to your goal. As the co-creator of your reality, take your life into your own hands. As you mount the Rainbow Bridge and tune into each part of yourself, you will gain a fuller realization of your true self. As all the parts of yourself become conscious, all the colors of the rainbow will merge into the One. As you enter the names of the deities, or saints, or the enlightened beings, of your path on your mandala, you can tell by the response of the energy that you get from the mandala whether the energy belongs there or not. You should feel good about the energy you feel from each of the eight places. Together, the combined energies should bring you into a quiet place inside yourself. If it doesn't, find where the imbalance is and correct it. You will know when you have corrected it, for you will find yourself in that still, quiet place inside yourself, where time stands still. Make the six circles on the mandala count to help bring some aspect of your life into consciousness. If you need more circles, add them. In the seventh place, the place of Wisdom, you get inspiration from higher self. Put there the name of the deity, saint, or enlightened being who is your guide and the source of your spiritual inspiration. This is a good place to start because it is the place of higher intuition, and is in tune with your higher self. Enter the names of the deities or divine beings that represent your spiritual Mother and Father. Enter the names of the deities, saints, or divine beings that best represent mastery over each aspect of your self and of your life, so that you can pray to them for help. In meditation, let them know you are setting up the mandala and seek their permission to work with them in this way. In working with the mandala, you are tuning into the energy of divine consciousness and being within yourself, and not to some entity outside you. If there is a dissonant energy present on the mandala, it will show itself by its very nature. Any internal spiritual

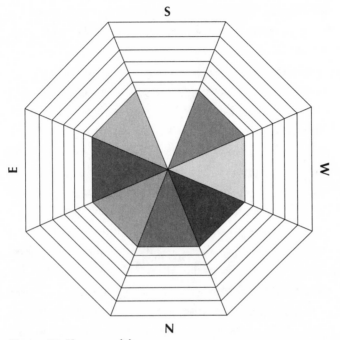

Figure 18. Your mandala.

connection that you have with the saints or deities should
be represented on the mandala for your highest good. If
you were born into a faith, but don't practice it now, you
should enter this on your mandala also. Enter the deities,
gods, or saints of that faith that relate to the eight energies
or eight aspects of yourself. If you don't know them, con-

sult a book to find the ones that best represent the eight energies for you, the ones you feel most comfortable praying to for help.

You are now working to bring all parts of yourself into union. This is a very important part of your life, which is now in your subconscious. You must retrieve and integrate this aspect of your life as well and bring it into union with yourself. You can pray to the angels and archangels for help, if you feel so inclined. The whole idea behind making a personal mandala is that it should represent the true you. It should bring the things that are important to you, that may now be in the darkness of your subconscious, into the light of consciousness. To come to a successful conclusion of the process requires that you have faith in the Great Mother, Spirit Father, or Universal Mind, the Creator—faith in yourself, free from fear or anger, and faith in the process of transformation. Then you can do whatever is necessary for a healing to take place within your being.

Keep a journal to record your realizations. If you work with a partner, or a circle of close friends who are fellow travelers, you can help each other come out of the darkness into the light.

As we have seen from the Way of the Tao, Earth plays a central part in our lives, along with the four elements or the four psychological types and the resultant thirty-two energies. Therefore, a connection with Earth is most advantageous. When you become connected to the Earth, you become connected at a basic level with all creation. A realization of this kind was given to a traveler to New Guinea. He and his brother were staying as guests of some friendly natives. The medicine man of the group told them that he would give one of them a realization before they left. A day or so before their departure, he called one of the brothers into his hut and sat with him in meditation. He gave him the realization that, in the great jungle, there is nothing to fear, since, in the jungle, there is only one tree because all the trees are connected at their roots. This gigantic tree is the home for all the animals and native peoples to live within. Likewise, in life, we ultimately come to realize there is nothing to fear, because we, like the, trees are all connected at our roots by spirit . . . by Tao.

20

The Paradigm Shift from Matter to Spirit

As ego or personality-self steps back and spirit-soul steps forward, you must truly accept this shift, initiated by higher self, to make it permanent. This is the grace, the miracle of higher self: connecting with your soul-self through your "I Am" or spirit. At this place, you open up to the shadow side of your reality. By acknowledging the existence of everyone and everything on the other side, and the right that they have to their existence, you establish the right to your own existence as well. This is working in tune with Divine Law; this is balancing the energy of both sides of consciousness so that you are freely flowing with the Tao. No matter what the external changes are in your life, you can remain balanced and centered internally. This is the internal initiation; this is when you become an initiate.

This initiation brings you consciously into Tai Chi, and you begin to open to and come in line with Divine Law. When you do, you find that the previous imbalances in your life just start to fall away. You see them there, but, since you are open to a higher law, they don't have any hold on you, so they just naturally fall away. This is the first step on the Way.

The Internal Shift in Reality

For some, preparing to take the next step into the Way involves a realization of what appears as the last "brick wall" in our way, God. We see this wall as part of the divine play of the Creator. As God is in everyone and orchestrating all of life's changes, you experience your disrupted life-conditions as part of the maze in the school of life God puts you through. Doors don't appear to open for you, and whenever difficulties begin to be resolved, some new trial or test comes your way. Understand that it is God, or Tao, working through all to bring you into your highest good. This wall you feel within is, in fact, no obstacle at all. Your individual reality is different from God's, so your reality is the obstacle. The Creator's reality is being in everyone, so everyone is a manifestation of the divine, and in his or her proper place for evolution. The Creator uses those in a seemingly better place to help those in a less fortunate place. That is the way God works. Some of us, however, have hardened our hearts toward others whom it would appear are obstructing our way. We feel that we have good cause but that's the fallacy of ego. To rectify this condition, add a new factor into your consciousness—that of time—and you will find that in time, everything is working itself out through evolution. If you allow yourself the facility to open up to the eternity of this moment, now, all will be well. If you let God, the divine, the Tao, come alive in your heart, in your mind, and in your life as higher self, you will feel the pressures of life's circumstances lifted from your being and feel more inclined to be freely in the flow. You need the Universal Law of Abundance to open for you and it will. Then the last obstacle will just naturally melt away.

In the dark night of the soul, you gain the ability to perceive things on a subconscious, as well as on a conscious, level. Just as the obstacles you perceived were on different levels, so is God. This extension of the last obstacle is merely the perception of God within all creation, but you are still not yet open to that energy as a part of your reality. You feel it within yourself, but you just don't seem to connect with it outside yourself. It is as though God were there, but hiding. This last bit of pain and suffering thus seems most acute, although it is mostly internal. You may wonder what you could have done to bring you to this state. You must recognize that in the paradigm shift from the material to spirit, your relationship with God has also made a shift to bring you into a relationship with God on a deeper level. For some, a relationship with God the Father shifts to the Mother–Father God, or Tao, and all of their offspring in creation—the divine within all creation. Everything is playing its part and everything is moving with evolution. You know the divine is in everything around you, but you can still feel the pain of separation, which makes it difficult to abide in the joy and bliss of love and compassion. You can't understand how you can perceive the divine in all that is around you, when all these bad things are still happening around you and to you. Although it might seem to be understandable that you get quite annoyed—even angry—with God and with life for all the bad things you feel that God still allows in your life, your anger is what continues to pull the bad things to you. You have to remember the Universal Law of energy response, which says that you attract the same energy vibration you give off. So anger pulls anger, love pulls love, compassion pulls compassion. Eventually, you will perceive the reality of this, that this is the way God works, and you are doing all of this to yourself. At this point, you can step back and release the anger. The anger is your need to hold onto your individual reality, which is keeping you from opening up to the larger reality of spirit. But you must understand this is part of the process of purification as well. How can you become pure without your soul going through the process of purification to come into spirit? With the dawn of a new age, we can expect to go through the fires of purification. So hold on, for what you are experiencing is just a part of the process. As you become purified, doors begin to open for you and difficulties naturally fall away—and with them, your anger.

Preparing to Take
the Second Step into the Way

At this point in the Way, you find your connection with higher self becoming firm. There are no more lapses in your internal contact. Sometimes you may find your internal contact is stronger than at others, but as long as you maintain your position as spirit-soul and view your life changes from that position, your higher self will have the time and the space to work things out in your life. As your position as spirit-soul pleases the Creator as higher self, you receive the grace of higher self. You will now be able to live through future changes in your life, while remaining centered in the Way, for your internal trust in your higher self has already been established. In this position, you will be tried and tested, so hold firm to your center.

The Second Step into the Way

As you come to the second step into the Way—what some call the Bodhisattva path—you enter the place of the initiate, a part of all spiritual paths. You realize that you are already in your new life and, for the first time in your life, things are working out for you. At the same time, however, you realize that if you do not do more, you will begin to slip back into ego consciousness. This realization brings you face to face with the Bodhisattva path of the initiate. The teaching is that, if you want to move forward, now you must give something back. This opens you up to your own unique Way, or Tao. This is the fifth discipline of self, or the Middle Way of divine grace to you. This is your dharma—how the divine, the Tao, God, chooses to manifest through you as your higher self. This represents your true purpose in life, your life work, your destiny, and how you fulfill your role in the divine plan.

When you agree to function in positive relationship with the divine, your role in the divine plan starts to become clear. You understand that, although you are living in the realm of free will, material life is centered in illusion. Although the material is the other half of the spiritual, if you go back to functioning from ego consciousness or personality-self, you will fall back into the illusion. You understand that, henceforth, you can only function from the position of higher self to be free. Thus, from your own free will, you and higher self become one and you become open to the Bodhisattva Way.

To internally acknowledge and accept the Way of the Bodhisattva in your life is to agree to function from the place of compassion for all. This is a covenant you make with the Creator. While walking your own unique Way or Tao, fulfilling your dharma and helping others when you can, your way becomes open before you. Going through this process, you will be made to know who you are by gaining a realization of many of your significant past lives, if they have not already been revealed. You will also come to realize who you are as higher self, and where you are going when you leave here after this lifetime. This removes all fear of death, and opens you up to experience life in its fullness, without attachment. It opens the way to spontaneity. Then you will function from the place of co-creator and find that Divine Law is working with you.

Let the energies of Tao, as yin and yang, manifest as divine love in your heart, and clear, golden-white light in through the top of your head. Let it manifest through the palms of your hands and the tips of your fingers, through the bottoms of your feet and through the tips of your toes. Let it manifest and radiate throughout your body and in the three tan tiens (head, heart, and gut), and in the fourth, as the golden-white flame from the top center of your head. Now open to Tao as divine love and be happy.

21

Journey Back Home

In this presentation of the Taoist path, I have tried to convey that you have within your self an energy vibration. That energy vibration is the God force, the Tao. If you can recognize that, in truth, you are this divine energy, you'll find that you will unleash a power that is very strong within yourself. This divine energy will bring you into attunement with all things that are around you. At the same time, all things that are around you will become a part of you. There is no universal way of spirituality; everyone has to walk in their own way to find their own consciousness of self, their own Tao. The path is like a bridge into a new dimension. When you step into the realm of Tai Chi, the realm of the heart linked by your enlightened mind or "I Am" as spirit, you create for yourself a sanctuary there. You create a place that you can call home. Home is a place within yourself where you can be yourself, where you can feel at ease, where you can feel free. It is there, as spirit-soul, that you can know the Great Soul—the Great Mother. You can know your higher self and become open to Spirit.

Tao

龍虎真心

天師

Chang Tao Ling
Guardian of the Way

Chang Tao Ling (see his teaching on page 234) took teachings from the major branches of Taoism and formed the Taoist religion, so, he is recognized as the patriarch of the lineage. Philosophical Taoism also recognizes Celestial Master Chang as a true realized being of Long Fu mountain, and the protector of the Way.

Appendix I
Taoist Meditation

Meditation is a conscious cessation of the stream of passive sensory perception, and the opening to thought consciousness as a sixth sense. This uncontrolled, extrasensory, automatic thought process makes for the highest level of creation. This is the place of the Wise Man, the Holy One of the *I Ching*, who sees through the seeds of fate and conducts himself centrally and in complete harmony with divine law.

Micro Cosmic Orbit

Begin by sitting with your back straight. Bring white light in at navel and bring down to root center, position 1 and

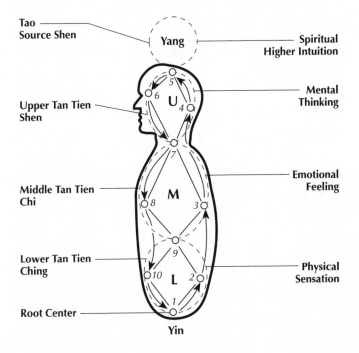

focus there. Keeping white light at position 1, move white light to position 2 and focus. Move white light to position 3 and focus. Continue up the back and down the front and focus white light at positions 4–10 to complete a round. Continue rounds and close at navel center. Tongue should be at the roof of mouth just behind front teeth during meditation. (Use golden white light like the Sun.)

Three Tan Tiens

Begin by sitting with your back straight. Bring the white light from navel to the lower tan tien and fill the whole lower tan tien with white light. Keeping the white light at the lower tan tien, now extend it to the upper tan tien and fill the whole upper tan tien with white light. Keeping the white light at the lower and upper tan tiens, now fill the whole middle tan tien with white light. Now fill the whole body with white light. Bring the light back to heart center and close.

Appendix II
Advanced Meditation

Micro Cosmic Orbit of Source

Begin by sitting with your back straight. Bring white light in at navel and bring down to root center position 1 and focus there. Continue up the back and focus white light at positions 2, 3, 4, and 5. Extend white light out the crown center and over the head and circle the source center clockwise (as seen looking down at the top of the head) and return to position 5. Continue down the front and focus at positions 6, 7, 8, 9, and 10. Continue rounds and close at navel center. Your ideal as higher self can be placed in source center over the head, in the heart and other centers. Place tongue at roof of mouth behind front teeth for meditation. (Use golden white light like the Sun.)

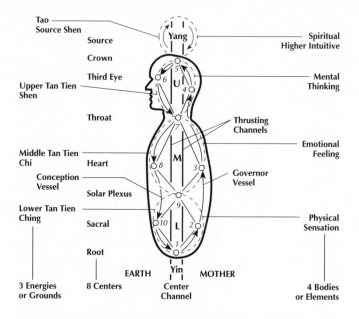

Tao — Source Shen

Source

Crown

Third Eye

Upper Tan Tien Shen

Throat

Middle Tan Tien Chi

Heart

Conception Vessel

Solar Plexus

Lower Tan Tien Ching

Sacral

Root

Yang

Spiritual Higher Intuitive

Mental Thinking

Thrusting Channels

Emotional Feeling

Governor Vessel

Physical Sensation

EARTH — Yin — MOTHER

| 3 Energies or Grounds | 8 Centers | Center Channel | 4 Bodies or Elements |

Opening Center Channel

This part of the meditation is for opening the center channel and the heart chakra, as well as for harmonizing yin and yang energies within your body. Begin by sitting with your back straight. Bring white light in at navel and fill lower tan tien. Keeping white light in lower tan tien, extend it up the back to fill the upper tan tien, then out the crown to fill the source center. Keeping white light at source center, and upper and lower tan tiens, extend white light down to middle tan tien and fill. Now open pillar of light to golden white light of Heaven and orange white light of Earth and blend. Open pillar of light as center channel to yang energy of Heaven and to Yin energy of Earth. Let them unite in heart center as love, and close.

Appendix III
Meditation on the
Four Elements as Four
Qualities of Energy

Meditate on the four elements as the four bodies by relating to the three tan tiens in the body, and the last one over your head. Begin by illuminating the lower tan tien with golden white light, symbolized by health, and let it manifest throughout your body. Then illuminate the middle tan tien with golden white light, symbolized by unconditional love. Have unconditional love in your heart for yourself—as spirit soul—and let it manifest throughout your body. Then illuminate the upper tan tien with golden white light, symbolized by compassion, and let it manifest throughout your body. Then illuminate the fourth tan tien over your head with golden white light symbolized by Tao or Spirit, and let it manifest throughout the body. You have the power to heal yourself, to love yourself, to have compassion for yourself and others, and be at peace in the Tao. As children, we all had a soft spot in the top of the head. That opening in the skull allowed our spirit-soul to commune with the Great Spirit, the all-that-is. As we grew older, it closed and we became disconnected and attached to ego, personality-self. Now we have to become reconnected to the Great Spirit, to the all-that-is, by acknowledging our connection.

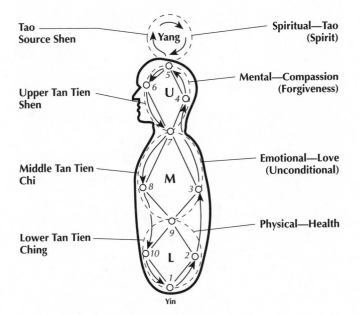

Bibliography

Beinfield, Harriet, L.Ac., and Efrem Korngold, L.Ac., O.M.D. *Between Heaven and Earth*. New York: Ballantine Books, 1991.

Blofeld, John. *Bodhisattva of Compassion*. London: Allen & Unwin, Ltd. 1977–8.

Campbell, Joseph. *On the Power of Myth with Bill Moyers: The Sacred Circle or Mandala*. Part 6 of 6. New York: Public Broadcasting System, June 27, 1988.

Cleary, Thomas. *The Inner Teachings of Taoism*. Boston: Shambhala Publications, 1986.

Dao, Deng Ming and The Wandering Taoist. *Seven Bamboo Tablets of the Cloudy Satchel*. San Francisco: HarperCollins, 1987.

Eliot, Alexander. *The Universal Myths*. New York: Penguin Putnam Inc., 1990.

Govinda, Lama Anagarika. *The Inner Structure of the I Ching*. Trumbull, CT: Weatherhill,1981.

Henricks, Robert G. *Lao Tze, Te Tao Ching*. New York: Ballantine Books, 1989.

Ho, Kwok Man and Joanne O'Brien. *The Eight Immortals of Taoism: Legends and Fables of Popular Taoism*. New York: Penguin Putnam, 1990.

Lao Tsu. *Tao Te Ching*. Translated by Gia-Fu Feng and Jane English. *Tao Te Ching, Lao Tzu*. New York: Vintage Books, 1972.

Lao Tzu. *Tao Te Ching*. Translated by Victor H. Mair. New York: Random House, 1990.

Ni, Hua-Ching. *The Book of Changes and the Unchanging Truth*. Santa Monica, CA: The Shrine of the Eternal Breath of Tao, 1983.

————. *The Complete Works of Lao Tzu: Hua Hu Ching*. Santa Monica, CA: The Shrine of the Eternal Breath of Tao, 1979.

Patte, Rowena. *Moving with Change*. New York: Arkana, 1986.

Schönberger, Martin. *The I Ching and the Genetic Code*. Santa Fe, NM: Aurora Press, 1979.

Yutang, Lin. *The Wisdom of Laotse (Tao Te Ching)*. New York: Modern Library, 1976.

Zweig, Connie and Jeremiah Abrams. *Meeting the Shadow*. New York: Jeremy P. Tarcher/Putnam, 1991